THE SUBSTANCE OF THE CHRISTIAN RELIGION

SOVNDLY SET FORTH in two bookes, by definitions and partitions, framed according to the rules of a naturall method by Amandus Polanus professor of Diuinitie.

The first booke concerneth faith.
The second concerneth good workes.
The principall pointes whereof are contained in a short table hereunto annexed.

Translated out of Latin into English by E. W.

This is life eternall, that they know thee to be the onely verie God, and him whom thou hast sent Iesus Christ. Ioh. 17.3.
Whatsoeuer I command you, take heede that you do it. Thou shalt put nothing therto, nor take any thing therfrō. Deu. 12.32.

AMANDUS POLANUS

Contents

TO THE READER 1
THE TITLES OF THE COMMON PLACES HANDLED IN THESE PARTITIONS. 3
THE FIRST BOOK OF THE PARTITIONS, AND DEFINITIONS OF DIUINITIE, FRAMED ACCORDING TO THE RULES OF A NATURALL METHODE, BY AMANDUS POLANUS OF POLANSDORF. 6

    Of Faith 6
    Hitherto we haue handled the simple attributes of God, which are of the first sort: they of the latter sort follow. 8
    Thus haue the simple attributes of God bene handled: The compared follow. 9
    Hitherto of the members attributed to God in the Scripture: now follow the senses. 10
    And these are the senses, which are attributed to God: the affections follow. 11
    And these are the affections which are attributed to God: the adioynts follow. 12
    Hitherto we haue spoken concerning the attributes of God: now we will speake concerning the persons of the Deitie. 12
    Hitherto concerning the essence of God: now concerning his workes. 13
    Hitherto generally concerning the benefites of God: now concerning his iudgements. 14
    Hitherto concerning the adiunctes of the workes of God, the sortes follow. 14
    Hitherto concerning Gods decree: now concerning the execution of Gods decree. 15
    Thus farre concerning perfect reason: now concerning perfect blessednesse. 16
    Hitherto concerning good Angels: now concerning euill Angels. 17
    Hitherto concerning Angels: now concerning man. 18
    Hitherto concerning the state of man: now concerning his will. 18
    Thus much concerning the will of man before the fall. 19
    Hitherto concerning the will of man being corrupted: now concerning the will of the regenerated man. 20
    Hitherto concerning the will of men in this life: now concerning their will in the life to come. 20

Hitherto concerning creation: now concerning the prouidence of God. 21
Thus much concerning good: now concerning euill. 21
Thus farre concerning the sinnes of deuils: now concerning the sinnes of men. 22
Thus much concerning the sinne of our first parents. 22
Thus much concerning originall sinne: now concerning Actuall sinne. 23
Thus farre concerning the euill of the offence: now concerning the euill of the punishment. 25
Thus much concerning the subiect of Gods prouidence: now concerning the parts thereof. 25
Thus far cōcerning Gods action done by meanes: now concerning Gods action without meanes. 27
Thus farre concerning the action of God: now concerning his permission. 27
Hitherto concerning the parts of Gods prouidence: the sorts follow. 28
Hitherto concerning the generall prouidence of God: his speciall prouidence followeth. 29
Hitherto concerning predestination: now concerning the naturall manifestation of God. 30
Hitherto concerning the naturall manifestation of God: now concerning afflaction. 30
Hitherto concerning the punishment: now concerning the crosse. ... 31
Thus farre concerning affliction: now concerning the secret mouing of the will. 32
Thus farre concerning the secret motion of the will: now concerning the gouerning of all wo dly or humane actions. 33
Hitherto concerning the generall workes of Gods speciall prouidence: the particular follow. 33
Thus farre concerning the threatening. 36
Hitherto concerning the second commandement: now concerning the third. 36
Hitherto concerning the first table of the ten commandements: The second followeth. 37
Hitherto concerning the explication of the ten commandements: now concerning the vses of the morall law. 38
Thus farre concerning Gods perpetuall law: now concerning the law of God for a certaine time. 39

Hitherto concerning the law of God, now concerning the Gospell.... 40
Thus farre concerning the natures in the person of Christ: now concerning his state. 40
Thus farre concerning the distinction of the natures in the personall vnion: now concerning the effects of the vnion. 41
Hitherto concerning the exaltation of the nature assumed: now concerning the communicating of the Idioms or properties. 42
Thus much concerning the personall vnion. 43
Thus farre concerning the incarnation of Christ: now concerning his obedience. 43
Hitherto of the euils which Christ suffered from his birth, euen to the last, and solemne acte of his Passion. 44
Thus farre concerning the striuing of Christ: now concerning his betraying. 45
Thus much concerning the betraying of Christ. 45
Hitherto concerning the passion of Christ: now concerning his death, and those things which followed his death, namely his burying, and descending into hell. 45
Hitherto concerning Christes humiliation: now concerning his exaltation. 46
There are foure endes and vses of the resurrection of Christ. 46
Hitherto concerning Christes ascension: now concerning his sitting at the right hand of God the father. 47
Hitherto concerning the person of Christ: now concerning his office. 47
Thus farre concerning the Propheticall office of Christ: now concerning his Priesthood. 48
Thus much concerning the expiation of sinne: now concerning intercession to God. 49
Hitherto concerning Christes Priesthood: now concerning the kingly office of Christ. 49
Thus farre concerning the reuelation of doctrine: now concerning the foretelling of things to come. 50
Hitherto concerning the absolute foretelling of things to come. 50
Thus much concerning the promise: now concerning the threatning. 51
Hitherto concerning the supernaturall manifestation of Gods will: now concerning his calling of vs. 52

Thus much concerning the outward calling: now concerning the inward. 52
Hitherto concerning our calling to Christ: now concerning our calling to some office. 52
Thus farre concerning our calling: now concerning Gods couenant. 52
Thus much concerning the couenant of workes: now concerning the couenant of grace. 53
Thus farre concerning the giuing of the holy spirite: now concerning our communion with Christ. 55
Thus farre concerning iustification: now concerning Regeneration. 56
Thus much concerning enlightening: now concerning repentance. . 57
Hitherto concerning the mortification of the old man: now concerning the quickening of the new man. 58
Thus far concerning the regeneratiō of the soule: now concerning the regeneration of the body. 58
Hitherto concerning the parts of regeneration: the perpetuall adioynts thereof remaine. 59
Hitherto concerning regeneration: now concerning adoption and the freedome of the sonnes of God. 59
Thus farre concerning adoption: now concerning the freedome of the sonnes of God. 60
Thus much concerning inward freedome: now concerning outward freedome. 60
Hitherto concerning our communion with Christ: now concerning our preseruation in this communion. 62
Hitherto concerning the common comfort in euery affliction: now concerning the particular comfort in death. 64
Hitherto concerning comfort: now concerning the rest of the benefites. 66
Hitherto concerning our preseruation in this communion with Christ: now concerning the gift of eternall life. 66
Hitherto concerning the promise of grace: now concerning the answering againe of a good conscience. 66
Hitherto concerning the eternall couenant: now concerning the temporall couenaur. 67
Hitherto concerning Gods couenant: now concerning the diuine signe. 67
Thus farre concerning a miracle: now concerning a Sacrament. 68

Hitherto concerning the sacrament of the couenant of workes: now concerning the Sacrament of the couenant of grace. 69
Hitherto concerning the earthly matter: now concerning the outwarde action in a Sacrament. 71
Hitherto concerning the action of the minister that administreth the Sacrament. 71
Hitherto concerning the parts of the couenant of the Sacrament of Grace: the ends follow. 73
Thus farre concerning the ends of the couenant of grace. 74
Thus farre concerning circumcision: now concerning the Passeouer. 75
Thus farre concerning the ordinary Sacraments of the old Testament: now concerning the extraordinary. 76
Hitherto concerning the Sacraments of the old Testament: now concerning the Sacraments of the new Testament. 76
Thus farre concerning the action of the Minister administring Baptisme: now concerning the actions of a faithfull man receiuing Baptisme. 77
Hitherto concerning Baptisme: now concerning the Lords Supper. .. 78
Hitherto concerning the earthly matter in the holy Supper: now concerning the outward action 81
Thus farre concerning the action of the minister: now concerning the outward action of a faithfull man vsing the holy Supper. 82
Hitherto concerning the receiuing of the bread and wine: now concerning thankesgiuing. 83
Thus farre concerning the parts of the Lordes Supper: now concerning the preparation of a faithfull man before the vse thereof. 83
Concerning the trying of a mans selfe before the vse of the Supper of the Lord. 84
Hitherto concerning the Sacrament of the eternall couenant: now concerning the Sacrament of the temporall couenant. 85
Thus farre concerning the workes of God which are done in this life: now concerning those workes which shall be done in the life to come. 85
Thus farre concerning the finall sentence to be pronounced to the elect: now concerning the finall sentence to be denounced against the reprobate. 87

Hitherto concerning the generall raysing vp of the dead, and the last iudgement: now concerning the manifestation of the glory of God to all eternitie. 87

Hitherto we haue layd open faith concerning God: now concerning the Church. 88

Thus farre concerning the vniuersall Church, now concerning the particular. 88

Hitherto concerning the Ministers of the church of the old Testament: now concerning the Ministers of the Church of the new Testament. 90

Hitherto concerning the extraordinarie Ministers of the Church of the new Testament: now concerning the ordinary. 91

Thus farre concerning the Ecclesiasticall ministery: now concerning the Ecclesiasticall power. 92

Hitherto concerning the power of order: now concerning the power of Iurisdiction. 92

Thus farre concerning the Ecclesiasticall punishment: now concerning absolution. 94

Hitherto concerning Pastors: now concerning Doctors. 94

Thus farre concerning Bishops: now concerning their helpers. 94

Hitherto concerning the gouernours: now concerning the disposers of the Church goods. 95

Thus farre concerning Deacons: now concerning Deaconesses. 95

Hitherto concerning the Ministers of the church: now concerning the hearers. 95

Thus farre concerning the proper gouernment of the church: now concerning the common. 95

Hitherto concerning the true church: now concerning the false Church. 97

Hitherto concerning the Iewes: now concerning the Gentiles. 97

And thus farre concerning open enemies: now concerning dissembled enemies. 98

Thus farre is shewed what Antichrist is: now who it is. 99

Thus farre concerning Antichrist himselfe: now concerning the Church of Antichrist. 99

So much concerning Antichrist: now concerning false Christs. 100

THE SECOND BOOKE OF THE DEFINITIONS AND PARTITIONS OF DIUINITIE, FRAMED ACCORDING TO THE RULES OF A NATURALL METHODE, BY AMANDUS POLANUS OF POLANSDORFE. 101

Of good workes. 101
So much concerning the feare of God: now concerning subiection vnto God. 102
Hitherto concerning the adioynts of good workes as they respect God. 103
Hitherto we haue spoken of the adioynts of good workes as in respect of our selues: now concerning the adioynts of good workes, in respect of our neighbour. 105
So much concerning the adioynts of good workes: their kinds follow. 105
Thus farre concerning humility: now concerning confidence in God. 107
So much concerning faith: now concerning hope in God. 109
So much concerning confidence: now concerning patience. 109
Hitherto concerning that worship of God which is only inward: now concerning that which is both inward and outward. 110
Thus much concerning the distribution of prayer: now concerning the forme of prayer. 111
This is the first part of the entrance: the second followeth. 112
So much concerning the entrance of the Lords prayer: the petitions follow. 113
The three former petitions haue been thus expounded: the three later follow. 114
Thus hath the second part of the Lordes prayer bene handled: the third followeth. 115
Hitherto we haue handled the third part of the Lords prayer: the conclusion remaineth. 116
Hitherto concerning prayer: now concerning an oath. 116
So much concerning calling vpon God: now concerning thankesgiuing. 117
And thus farre concerning thankesgiuing: now concerning the confession of the truth. 118
Hitherto concerning the confession of the truth: now concerning the obseruing of the Ecclesiasticall rites or ceremonies. 120

Hitherto concerning the sanctification of an holy day: now concerning a godly fast.	120
So much concerning a fast: now concerning a vow.	121
Hitherto concerning a rite common to the old and new Testament: now concerning that that is proper to either of them.	121
Hitherto concerning-sacrifices: now concerning the obseruation of holy times.	122
Hitherto concerning the holy times of a day: now concerning the holy times of a yeare.	122
Hitherto haue the solemnities instituted by God himselfe bene handled.	123
Hitherto concerning the yearly solemnities.	123
Hitherto concerning the publicke rites of the old Testament: now concerning the priuate.	124
Hitherto we haue handled the rites proper to the old Testament: the rites proper to the new Testament remaine to be treated of.	124
Hitherto concerning the holy dayes of Christ.	124
And thus farre concerning the worship of God: now concerning vertue.	125
Hitherto concerning continency: now concerning thriftinesse.	126
Thus farre concerning Temperance: now concerning the care or desire of true glory.	126
Hitherto we haue spoken of vertue which is referred to our selues: now concerning vertue towards others.	126
Hitherto concerning ciuility: now concerning brideling the inordinat motions of the mind.	128
So much concerning the brideling of pride: now concerning the brideling of anger.	129
Hitherto concerning the brideling of anger: now concerning the brideling of the desire, or couetousnesse.	130
Hitherto concerning the brideling of the inordinate motions of the mind: now concerning Christian loue.	130
So much concerning liberalitie in communicating of riches.	131
Thus farre concerning liberalitie: now concerning friendship.	132
Hitherto concerning friendship: now concerning a fellowlike feeling.	132
Thus farre concerning a fellowlike feeling towards the liuing: now towards the dead.	132

So much concerning a fellowlike feeling: now of the procuring of other mens good. 133
Hitherto concerning loue: now concerning iustice. 133
Hitherto concerning priuate iustice in a mans owne vocation. 134
And thus we haue spoken concerning error, which ought to be farre from the consent of the bridegrome and the bride: now concerning compulsion. 136
The consent of the bridegrome & bride hath bin handled: now concerning the consent of others that haue interest and right therein. 136
So much concerning the consent which is required to wedlocke: now followeth what persons be fitte. 137
So much concerning those vvho may be ioyned together, as hauing power to bring foorth issue. 138
So much concerning the line: now concerning the degree. 139
The account of the degrees hath beene handled, now followeth the forbidding of wedlock in respect of the degrees. 141
Hitherto we haue spoken of alies by nature or by bloud: now of allies by mariage. 142
Thus farre concerning the betroathings which ought to goe before wedlocke: now concerning the duties of wedlocke or mariage. 142
And thus the maner of proceeding in the case of adultery ought to be framed and ordered: the maner of proceeding in the case of forsaking, now followeth to be handled. 144
Hitherto we haue spoken concerning the maner of proceeding in diuorcement: now we must speake of the time after which another wedlock may be graunted to the innocent person. 144
Hitherto concerning common iustice of both the maried parties: now of that that is proper to one of them. 145
Hitherto concerning the iustice of mariage: now concerning the education of children. 145
Hitherto concerning the holinesse of wedlock: now touching the disposing of houshold affaires or matters. 146
A iustice as pertaining to a houshold or familie hath bin thus set forth: ciuill iustice doth now follow. 146
Hitherto concerning ciuill distributiue iustice, which ought to be exercised towards euery one: now followeth that which is to be exercised towards some fewe. 147

Thus farre concerning thankefulnesse: now concerning submission. 147
Hitherto concerning distributiue iustice: now concerning commutatiue iustice...148
Hitherto concerning priuate iustice: now concerning publike iustice. 148
Thus farre concerning the iustice of the magistrate in peace: now concerning iustice in warre. 149
The end of the second booke of the Definitions and partitions of Diuinitie...149
TO THE GENTLE READER HEALTH IN CHRIST. 149

To the Reader

TO THE RIGHT HONORABLE AND HIS VERIE GOOD LORD, THE LORD Edward Earle of Bedford: and to the right honorable also and vertuous Ladie, the Ladie Lucie his wife, E. W. wisheth all growth of goodnesse in this life, and in the end euerlasting blessednesse through Christ.

MAy it please your HH. to vnderstand, that hauing by my fathers appointmēt for exercise sake, according to my poore skill, translated out of Latin into English, this worthy worke following: and God hauing besides prepared a way (when I did neither thinke nor know of it) to bring it to light & sight of men, by putting it into Print, I bethought my selfe, as well as my want of yeares & discretion would suffer me, of some worthy persons & patrōs to whom I might dedicate these my simple labours. Amōgst many none came more oftē & more iustly into my remēbrance, thā your HH. whose affectiō in the Lord to my father, and some measure of Christian care for me in the world, haue made me bold, & euen as it were to presume, to dedicate these simple fruits of my first trauailes vnto you. What reasons I haue besides those alledged to lead me thereto, I shall not need largely to lay out. Your HH. zeale to Religion: your fauours to me, as also some declaration of all dutifull thankefulnesse from my selfe towards you for the same haue greatly prouoked me. In whō though there be nothing as in regard of my selfe and paines taken herein, that may commend it, yet as in respect of the worke it selfe, sure I am, not by mine owne iudgement I protest (for how weake and childish that is, I very well know) but by the sentence of sundry very learned men, both for the soundnesse and sufficiencie of the things therein contained, as also for the methodicall maner of handling the same, there will be found much that may well beseeme your HH. profession and place. And so earnestly praying the good acceptation of that which is done, that vnder your HH. patronage it may be the better receiued amongst men: and humbly beseeching the continuance of your HH. fauours, that so I may the better proceede in godlinesse and learning, whereunto my parents, though not able indeede of themselues to maintaine me therein, haue vnfainedly dedicated me, & I my self haue willingly vowed my selfe; and hartily crauing pardon for my boldnesse & scapes this or any other way cōmitted, I humbly end.

At Londō the first of this Ianuarie. 1595.

Your HH. humble and dutifull as he is much bound. Elijahu Wilcocks.

The Titles of the Common Places Handled in These Partitions.

- 1 Of the word of God pag. 1, 98.
- 2 Of God. pag. 5.
- 3 Of the attributes of God. pag. 5.
- 4 Of the persons of the Deitie, or of the holie Trinitie. pag. 10
- 5 Of the workes of God. pag. 11.
- 6 Of the decree of God, where also of the decree of Predestination. pag. 12
- 7 Of Creatiō, where of the image of God. pag. 13.
- 8 Of good and euill Angels. pag. 15.
- 9 Of man, his state and free will. pag. 16-18.
- 10 Of the prouidence of God. pag. 19.
- 11 Of good. pag. 19.
- 12 Of euill. pag. 19.
- 13 Of sinne pag. 20ff.
- 14 Of the action of God. pag. 23.
- 15 Of the instruments of God. pag. 25.
- 16 Of Gods permission or sufferance. pag. 25.
- 17 Of the conseruation of things. pag. 26.
- 18 Of Predestination. pag. 27.
- 19 Of the naturall manifestation of God, where concerning the law of nature. pag. 28.
- 20 Of afflictions & the crosse. pag. 28ff.
- 21 Of Gods secret mouing of the wills. pag. 30.
- 22 Of Gods gouerning of all humane actiōs. pag. 30.
- 23 Of the supernaturall manifestation of Gods will. pag. 31.
- 24 Of the law of God whereof the decalogue or 10. Cōmandemēts. 31ff.
- 25 Of the ceremoniall and iudiciall law of God. pag. 37.
- 26 Of the Gospell. pag. 37.
- 27 Of Christ, of his person, of his double state, incarnation, conception by the holy spirit, of his personall vnion, of the maiestie of the humane nature of Christ, of the cōmunicating of the Idioms, or properties of his birth, obediēce, suffering, death, burying, descēsion to hell, exaltation, resurrection from the dead, ascension into heauen, sitting at the right of God his father. pag. 37ff.
- 28 Of the office of Christ, or of the office of the Mediatour. pag. 45ff.

- 29 Of the foretelling of things to come. pag. 47.
- 30 Of Gods promises. pag. 48.
- 31 Of Gods threatnings. pag. 49.
- 32 Of Gods calling. pag. 49.
- 33 Of the couenant of God. pag. 50.
- 34 Of the benefits purchased to vs by Christ. pag. 51.
- 35 Of the cōmuniō or fellowship with Christ. pag. 52.
- 36 Of iustification, where of forgiuenesse of sinnes. 52.
- 37 Of regeneration or sanctification, where of repentance. pag. 54ff.
- 38 Of adoption. pag. 57.
- 39 Of the libertie of the sonnes of God, where of Christian libertie, and of things indifferent. pag. 57ff.
- 40 Of comfort vnder the crosse, & in death. pag. 61ff.
- 41 Of diuine signes, where of miracles and the Sacraments. pag. 64ff.
- 42 Of Baptisme. pag. 74.
- 43 Of the Supper of the Lord. pag. 75ff.
- 44 Of the workes of God after this life, where of the generall resurrectiō, & the last iudgement, and glorification of the elect. pag. 83ff.
- 45 Of the true Church, where of true Religion. pag. 85ff.
- 46 Of the Ministers of the Church. pag. 88.
- 47 Of the Ecclesiasticall power, where of the power of order & iurisdiction, of the lawfull calling of Ministers, of the power of the keyes, of the Ecclesiasticall discipline, of excōmunication. pag. 89ff.
- 48 Of Counsels. pag. 93.
- 49 Of the false Church, where of false Religiō, of the enemies of Christ and his kingdome, of the Iewes, & of their reiection and restitutiō, of the Mahumetistes, heretickes, Anrichrist, of the Church of Antichrist, and of false Prophets. 94ff.

The second booke.
- 50 Of good workes. pag. 98.
- Of things adioyned thereto. pag. 99ff.
- 51 Of things disagreeing with good workes, where of the feare of God, of constancie, prudence, zeale, fortitude, the glorie of God. pag. 99ff.
- 52 Of the inward & outward worship of God, & the things that disagree therefrom, where of liuely faith. 102ff.
- 53 Of inuocation, where of prayer, of the Lords prayer, of an oath. pag. 107ff.

- 54 Of thankesgiuing, and the confession of truth. pag. 113ff.
- 55 Of the rites or ceremonies of the Church, where of a godly fast, vow, sacrifices of the old Testament & feast. pag. 117ff.
- 56 Of vertue, where concerning the desire of wisdome, of fortitude, temperance, chastitie, liberalitie, iustice, and the whole company of vertues. pag. 102ff.
- 57 Of priuate iustice, where of wedlocke, and of diuorse. pag. 129.
- 58 Of the publike iustice, where of Magistrate and lawes, of peace and warre. pag. 145ff.

The First Book of the Partitions, and Definitions of Diuinitie, framed according to the Rules of a Naturall Methode, by Amandus Polanus of Polansdorf.

Of Faith.

THe word of God, is a doctrine written by the Prophets and Apostles, the holy spirite being the inditour thereof, perfectly deliuering the way how to obtaine eternall life. 2. Pet. 1.21. Ephes. 2.20. Iohn. 5.24.39. and 20.29.31. 1. Cor. 1.21. 2. Tim. 1.10. and 2.5. Tit. 1.1. 2. Rom. 1.16. Psal. 32.1. and 1.1. and 119.1. and so forward. Mat. 5.3. & so forward. Iam. 1.21.22.

Of the word of God there be two partes: the first concerning faith. Act. 24.14.15.16. Rom. 1.16. Hab. 2.4. the other cōcerning good workes. Iam. 2.20. Phil. 1.27. Tit. 3.8. Mar. 1.15. 1. Tim. 1.18.19.

The first part, namely concerning faith, doth teach vs, what we must beleeue to saluation. And that cōcerneth either God, or the Church.

God, is an eternall, infinite, omnipotent, and most holy spirit. Iohn 4.24. Psal 9.2. & 92.8. & 102.13. Esa. 63.16. Dan. 6.26. Heb. 1.12. Reu. 4.8. & 11.17. & 16.5. 1. Kin. 8.27. 2. Chro. 6.18. Iob. 11.7.8. Iere. 23.23. Psal. 139.7.10. Esa. 6.3. Gen. 17.1. & 35.11. Exod. 6.3. Deut. 7.8. & 10.17. Num. 11.23. Esa. 40.12. Matt. 19.26. Luk. 1.37. Reu. 1.8. Mat. 19.17. 2. Chr. 30.18.

Of the knowledge of God, or of faith concerning God, are two parts, the first concerning the essence of God, the second concerning his workes.

The essence of God, is the nature of God, whereby God is indeede, and doth subsist.

And that essence is but one: and therefore God is but onely one also.

There are two partes of the knowledge of the essence of God, the first concerning the attributes of God, the second concerning the distinction of the persons.

The attributes of God, are those titles, which are attributed to God, to declare his essence better vnto vs.

The attributes of God, are either simple, or compared.

The simple attributes of God are the esential properties of God, which doe agree to him without comparison.

Of these some haue such a similitude of him, as is in the creatures by creation: some haue not.

Of the former kind are blessednes, immortalitie, vnderstanding, praescience, memorie, will, goodnesse, holinesse, iustice, clemencie, long sufferance, patience, constacie, fortitude, truth, faithfulnesse, and the rest.

The goodnesse of God is that, by which he hath bene euerlastingly contented with him selfe, not hauing neede of any other thing. 1. Tim. 1.11. & 6.15.

The vnderstāding of God, is that by which he hath a perfect vnderstāding of al things, & this is somtimes called the wisdome of God.

The immortalitie of God, is that by which he neuer dieth. 1. Tim. 1.17. & 6.16.

The praescience of God, is a most perfect foreknowledge of all things to come.

The memorie of God, is that by which he doth most exactly remember all things. Psal. 25.6.7. Esa. 49.16.

The will of God, is that by which he willeth all things. Rom 9.15.22. Eph. 1.5.9.11.

And that will is onely one, & most simple if we respect God him self, but so farre as we respect mē, to whō it is either reuealed or hid, it is two fold: manifest or secret. The schoolemen do call the former of these, the wil of the signe, the other the will of the good pleasure of God.

The secret wil also in due time appointed by God, is made open and manifest.

The will of God is most free, whereupon also it is called the free will of God.

The free wil of God, is that self same essence of God, vnderstanding by it selfe all things immediatly and most perfectly, & that most freely, but yet vnchangeably and necessarily, willing that which is good onely, and abhorring that onely which is euill, neither depending of another former beginning, but of it selfe onely. And this alone may properly be called of his owne power.

The goodnes of God is that by which he is the author of all good things.

And he doth exercise this, either generally towards all creatures, or else particularly towards his elect.

The former is called beneficence, the later is called mercie.

The beneficence of God, is that by which he giueth his gifts to all his creatures. Mat. 5.44.45. Act. 14.17.

The mercie of God is that by which God doth good to his elect, although they deserue nothing of him but euill. Esa. 49.10.13. Eph. 2.3.4. Psal. 145.9.

The holinesse of God is that by which he doth altogether abhorre all impuritie & vncleanesse Esa. 6.3. Reu. 4.8. Ierem. 3.12.

The iustice of God, is that by which he dealeth iustly in all things. Psal. 116.11. Rom. 3.4.

The clemencie of God, is that by which he doth represse his anger, which is most iust, that he might spare vs. Exod. 34.5.

The long sufferance of God, is that wherby he doth a long time defer his anger, and punishment against sinners, that he might prouoke them to repentance. Exod 34.5.

The patiēce of God is that by which he suffereth a long time patiently the sins of men, that he might lead thē to repentance. Esa. 48.9

The constancie of God, is that by which he performeth most certainely that which hee hath spoken. Exod. 34.5.

The fortitude of God, is that by which he is able to performe all thinges that hee doth wil. 1 Sam. 2.2. 2 Sam. 23.13. Esay. 28.2. & 49.26. Ier. 50.34. Reuel. 18.8.

The truth of God is that by which hee speaketh and doeth all things as they are indeed, he himselfe being most free from all lying. Rom. 3.4. Deut. 7.9.

The fayhfulnes of God is that by which he most faythfully performeth to his children that which hee hath promised. Esay. 49.7. Exod. 34.6. Deut. 7.10.

<u>Hitherto we haue handled the simple attributes of God, which are of the first sort: they of the latter sort follow.</u>

The simple attributs of God, of the later sort are those which haue not in thē such a similitude of him, as is in some creatures by creatiō.

Of which sort are these, Eternitie, Infinitnes, vbiquity, omnipotency, omniscience.

Eternitie, is an essential propertie of God, by which hee is sayde to bee without any beginning or ending. Esa. 43.13. Ps. 90.2. & 92.8.

Infinitenesse, is an essentiall propertie of God, by which we vnderstand that the diuine essence can in no wise be cōprehēded in any boundes. 1. Kin. 8.27. 2. Chro. 2.6. and 6.18.

It is also called his vnmeasurablenesse.

Vbiquitie is an essentiall property of God, by which he is alwayes present euery where in all things. Iere. 23.23.24. Psal. 139.7.10. Esa. 6.3. and 66.1.

It is also called omnipresence.

Infinitnesse is the cause of vbiquitie.

For that that is euery where, is therfore euery where, because it is infinite. Neither is, neither can any thing be said to be euery where, except it be infinit.

And this is proper to the Deitie alone, that it be whole euery where & in euery particular place.

Omnipotencie, is an essentiall propertie of God, by which he can bring to passe all things, whatsoeuer he doth will now he doth will all those things, which are agreable to his nature and word. Luk. 1.37. and 18.27.

Omniscience, is an essentiall propertie of God, by which he most perfectly knoweth, euen in one moment all things euery where. Hebr. 4.13.

The meditation hereof hath a double vse, one for our exhortation, the other for our comfort.

It serueth vs for exhortation, because it stirreth vs vp to the sincere feare of God, that in euery place we may flie all filthinesse, and sins, seeing all things though neuer so secret are subiect to the eyes of God, & nothing can be hid frō thē: seing also God will bring forth into the open light all secrets in due time.

It serueth vs for comfort, because it doth strēgthē our minds in all miseries, seeing God knoweth them, & they cānot be hid frō him.

Thus haue the simple attributes of God bene handled: The compared follow.

The compared attributs of God are those titles which do belong properly to creatures, but are by a metaphore or similitude attributed to God. For the Scripture oftentimes doth speake of God, according to mās capacitie.

Of them some are taken from man, some from other creatures.

Those which are taken from man, are said to be attributed to God, by a humane passiō. A humane passion is a metaphore, whereby those things which perteine to man, are by a similitude attributed to God.

Of this sort are these, the parts, members, senses, affections, and adioynts of man.

The soule which is a part of man, is attributed to God Iere. 5.29. and 9.9. Amos. 6.8.

Where by the soule is meāt, the life of God, that is to say, the very essence of God it selfe.

And by the members of the body, by the senses, affectiōs & adioynts, which are attributed to God, a power is meant to be in God, performing for vs certaine actiōs by an incōprehensible maner, whereof the works which men performe by the meanes of their members, senses, affections and adioyntes be as it were a certaine resemblance.

These members of the body are attributed to God: the head, the face, the eye, the apple of the eye, the mouth, the eare, the nose the nostrels, the hand, the arme, the right hand, the finger, the hart, the wombe, the feete.

By Gods head is meant God himself being such a one as to whose glory all things are to be referred, which are subiect to him in Christ 1. Cor. 11.3. God is the head of Christ.

By face or countenance, is meant sometime presence, sometimes the fauour & kindnesse or God. Psal. 114.7. and 27.8.9. and 31.17. Sometimes anger. Psal. 34.17.

By the eyes is meant, either the good will and fauor of God. Psal. 34.16. Or the prouidence of God: or else this, namely that God seeth all things.

By the apple of the eye is meant, that which is most deare to God. Deut. 32.10. Psal. 17.8. Zach. 2.8.

By the mouth is meant either the decree of Gods prouidēce. Mat. 4.4. or else the cōmandement or reuealing of his word. Iere. 9.12.

By the eares is meant, either readinesse, and facilitie in hearing our prayers. Psal. 31.3. and 34.16. Or this, that God heareth all things.

By the nose is meant the fierce wrath of God. Ierem. 49.37.

By the nostrels to which smelling is attributed is meant, that acceptation by which he taketh sacrifices to be well pleasing, and acceptable vnto him. Genes. 8.21.

By the hand is meant power, protection, liberalitie, workemanship, and those things which are like these. Iob. 10.8. Psal. 31.6. & 8.7.

By the arme is meant power, strength and might. Genes. 49.24. Exod. 6.6.

By the right hand, is meant, the power, or rule of God. As in the Creede of the Apostles.

By the finger is meant, power, mightie working. Exod. 8.19. or else workemanship. Exod. 31.18.

By the hart is meant, either the liuing essence of God, for the hart is iudged to be the seate of life in a liuing creature. Genes. 6.6. or the decree of God, because the holy Scripture doth appoint the hart to be the seate of the sense, whose part is to think, & to determine. Iere. 19.5. or the good pleasure of God, as when Dauid is said to be a man according to Gods owne hart.

By the wombe is meant generation. Psal. 110.3.

By the feete is meant strength or power. Psal. 110.1. or else the presence of God.

<u>Hitherto of the members attributed to God in the Scripture: now follow the senses.</u>

By the senses attributed to God there is vnderstood the prouidēce of God. Mat. 14.2.

The senses which are attributed to God, are either inward or outward.
Inward, as memorie or remembrance. Esa. 49.16. 1. Sam. 15.2.
To which is opposed forgetfulnesse. Esa. 49.14.
The outward senses attributed to God are sight. Genes. 1.4.
Hearing. Psal. 5.2. and 6.8.9.
Smelling. Genes. 8.21.

<u>And these are the senses, which are attributed to God: the affections follow.</u>

Affections are attributed to God, as loue, grace, or mercy, anger, furie, hatred repēting.

The loue of God, is that whereby he being moued doth bestow his gifts on his creatures. Mal. 1.2.3. Iohn. 2. Tit. 3.4 Ephes. 2.4.

The grace or mercy of God, is the fauour, good will, & clemencie of God, by which he giueth freely to his elect without any desert of theirs, all good things both for body and soule, especially eternall life. Rom. 11.6.12.25.

The schoolemen do make two sorts of the grace of God: A grace making a man freely accepted, & another grace giuen freely: The schoolemen for the most part do vnderstand by the grace which maketh a man freely acceptable, the gifts & qualities infused into the soule: but more rightly it is taken for the fauour, & mercy of God, which doth not consist in vs but in God himselfe.

Grace giuē freely, is euery gift which doth proceede from the loue, & liberalitie of God, and is bestowed vpon vs. Paule calleth it the gift by grace. Rom. 5.15. Schoolemen call it an infused grace.

The good pleasure of God, is that by which he suffereth all good things to please him, Gene. 1. God saw all things that he had made, and behold they were very good. So workes done by faith please God.

The anger of God, are those punishments, by which he punisheth sinnes. Rom. 1.18.

And that is also called the reuengement of God. Esa. 47.3. Psal. 2.5.

The furie of God, is the fierce and mighty wrath of God declared by most grieuous punishments. Psal. 2.5.12.

The hatred which is in God, is an abhorring lothing and reiecting of euill. Mala. 1.2.3. Rom. 9.13.

The repenting of God, is not a changing of his diuine counsell and decree, which is immutable. 1. Sam. 15.29. but a chaunging of the workes of God. Genes. 6.6. 1. Sam. 15.11. Ierem. 18.8

The causes thereof are either the sinnes or repentance of men.

Notwithstāding this kind of change is decreed by God from euerlasting. For God hath decreed both of these, namely to performe some worke, and to change it againe, for the sinnes, & repentance of men. That changing of the worke is called the repenting of God.

And these are the affections which are attributed to God: the adioynts follow.

The adioynts of man which are attributed to God are these, to sit in a throne to see. Psal. 2. to arise, to ascēd, to descēd, apparell. Psal. 104.2. he is called also a husbandman. Iohn. 15.1.

And these attributes are taken from mā others follow, which are both common & also taken from other creatures: Of this sort are these, place, time, ascending, descending.

Wings are also attributed to God, by which is meant protection and defence. Deut. 32.10. Psal. 17.8. Psal. 91.4.

Likewise a shadow is attributed to God. Psal. 91.1 by which is meant protection. For euen as a shadow doth protect vs from the beames, and heat of the sunne: so God doth protect vs from daungers.

So God by a metaphore is called by diuers names.

He is called a tower. Psal. 91.2. For euen as in high and defenced towers, we are safe from the enemy: so God doth set vs in safetie.

He is called, a shield, a buckler. Psal. 3.4.

He is called, a consuming fire. Deut. 4.24. & 9.3. Heb. 12.19.

He is called a rocke. Psal. 71.

He is called a strōg dwelling place. Psal. 71.3.

He is called a defence. Psal. 71.3.

Hitherto we haue spoken concerning the attributes of God: now we will speake concerning the persons of the Deitie.

A person of the Deitie, is a subsistence in the Deitie, hauing such properties, as cannot be communicated from one to another.

There are three persons in the Deitie, the Father, the Son, & the holy ghost. Mat. 3.16. & 28.19. 1. Iohn. 5.7. Ephes. 2.18. Gene. 1.26. and 18.2. Exod. 3.6. and 15.16. Psal. 33.6. Esa. 6.3.

These are coeternall, and equall, of one, & the selfe same simple essence, distinct one frō another by an incommunicable proprietie. And those are distinguished one from another, not essentially, because the essence of them is but one, yet notwithstanding really: they differ from the essence of God, not in deed, but by respect or by relation onely.

The Father, is the first in the Godhead, which hath begot the Sonne frō euerlasting. Psal. 2.2. Cor. 13.

The Sonne, is the second in the Godhead, which is begotten of the Father, by an eternall communicating of the whole essence. Iohn. 1.14.18.34. and 3.16. Mat. 3.17. 2. Cor. 1.19. Hose. 11.3. Luke. 1.31. Rom. 1.4.

The diuine essence neither doth beget, neither is begotten: because that which doth beget is in very deed, distinguished from that which is begottē: now the diuine essence, being but one, and most simple, it cannot be distinguished from it selfe.

The Sonne, is beggotten of the essence of the Father: and hath the whole essence of the Father not by flowing from, neither by cutting out of the Father, neither by propagation, (for the essence of the Sonne, doth not flow from the essence of the Father, neither is it propagated or cut out of it) but by cōmunicating. And the Sonne is not in deede the Sonne of himselfe, because he is the Sonne of the Father: yet notwithstanding he is God of himselfe, that is to say, that essence which is in the Sonne, is not of another, but of it selfe, seeing the essence of the Father, and the Sonne, is one and selfe same. The essence of the Father, is of it selfe, without all beginning: but the essence of the Son, is the essence of the Father. For the Godhead, by which the Son is God, is that same by which the Father is God: therefore the essence of the Sonne is of it selfe and without beginning. Therefore Christ is God of himselfe. For except he be God of himselfe, he certainly can not be God at all. For that he be God, God hath it of himselfe naturally. He cannot be God whose essence is not of it selfe.

But it is one thing for the essence to be begotten, and another thing to be begotten of the essence. The essence is not begotten of the essence, the essence is without generation.

Therefore the Sonne also as he is God, is not begotten. But the Son is begotten of the essence of the Father. Wherefore Christ as he is God is of himselfe, as he is the Sonne, he is of the Father.

The holy Spirit is the third person in the Godhead, which proceedeth from the Father and the Sonne. Iohn. 15.25.26. and 20.22. Rom. 8.9. Esa. 6.8.9. Actes. 28.25.26. & 5.3.4. 1. Cor. 3.6. and 19.20 2. Cor. 6.16.

Therefore God is one in essence. Exod. 3.14. Deut. 4.35. and 6.4. and 7.9. and 10.17. and 32.39. 1. Cor. 12.6. Gal. 3.20. Ephes. 4.6. 1. Tim. 2.5. But three in persons, whereupon we worship the reuerend Trinitie, or Trinitie in vnitie. Genes. 1.26. and 18.2. 1. Iohn. 5.7. Ephes. 2.18. Rom. 9 5. 1. Timot. 3.16. Actes. 5.3.4.

<u>Hitherto concerning the essence of God: now concerning his workes.</u>

The works of God, are those things which God doth for his own glory. Psal 8.1. & 19. & 104.1. Prouerb. 16.4. Esay 48.9. Rom. 1.20.21.

And by the cōsideratiō of Gods works, diuers names are giuē to God in the Scripture.

Furthermore those are the vndeuided workes of the Trinitie, & yet we must keepe the personall proprietie, the naturall distinction, & order of the persons in working. For as the Son is of the Father, and the holy Spirite of the Father and the Sonne: so the Father worketh immediatly by the Sonne: and the Father and the Sonne, by the holy Spirite, in performing the same worke. For the Father is powerfull, but by the Sonne and the holy Spirite. Iohn. 5.19.

The Father worketh by the Son, not as by an instrument or helper of the working.

The workes of God, are either benefits, or iudgements.

The benefits of God, are the works which God doth performe for our good.

The benefites of God, are either spirituall, or bodily.

Spirituall benefites, are those which pertaine to the soule or spirituall life.

Bodily benefites, are those which pettaine to a bodily life.

Hitherto generally concerning the benefites of God: now concerning his iudgements.

The iudgements of God, are those works, by which he iustly layeth afflictiōs vpō men.

Againe the workes of God are either eternall, or limited in time.

The eternall works of God are those which were done from eternitie, before the foundations of the world were layd.

The workes of a certaine or set time, are those which are done in the time appointed.

Hitherto concerning the adiunctes of the workes of God, the sortes follow.

The workes of God are two: the decree of God, and the execution of Gods decree.

The decree of God, is the eternall and vnchangeable worke of God, whereby he hath decreed in himselfe, all things which he will do, & permit to be done, and all the circumstances of all things. Act. 2.23. and 4.28. & 10.42. Ephes. 1.1.5.11.

All things therefore are done by the decree of God. Ephes. 1.11. Mat. 6.33.

And God hath so decreed all things, that he hath determined the time, place, and the manner how they should be done: and also hath appointed al things particularly to their end: and hath moreouer ordained euen the very meanes, by which they shall come to that end.

Now the decree of God is vnchangeable, and vnmoueable, and such a one as God can not repent him of it, and therefore it is necessary. Psal. 33.11. Num. 23.19. 1. Sam. 15.29. Esa. 46.10. Mal. 3.6. Iam. 1.17. Esa. 14.24.27.

The decree of God, is either generall, or speciall.

Gods generall decree, is that which pertaineth generally to all and euery thing, great and small, yea, euen to those things, which fall out euery moment.

Gods speciall decree, is that which doth specially concerne men.

That pertaining properly to the eternall saluation, or destruction of men, is called the decree of Predestination.

The decree of Predestination, is the decree of God, concerning the eternall saluation, or destruction of men.

And that is two fold: the decree of electiō, or the decree of reprobation.

The decree of election, is that decree, by which God hath purposed with himselfe, to deliuer (and also to ordaine to eternall life, and that to the prayse of his glorious grace from that common destruction into which men would willingly haue thrust themselues headlong) all those whō he would haue mercy vpon. Ephes. 1.5. Mat. 22.14. Rom. 8.28. and 9.21. Act. 13.48. Luke. 10.20. Phil. 4.3. Reuel. 3.5. and 21.27.

The decree of election is by a metaphore called the booke of life, in which are written the names of those that shalbe saued. Reuel. 20.12.15.

The decree of reprobation, is that decree by which God hath purposed with himselfe to leaue, and that for the declaration of his iustice, those on whom he will not take pitie, in euerlasting destruction, to which, for their sinnes, they should be subiect. Prouerb. 16.4. Exod. 9.16. Rom. 9.22. 2. Pet. 2.4. Iob. 4.18. and 15.15. Iude. vers. 4. Reuel. 13.8. and 17.8. and 20.15.

Hitherto concerning Gods decree: now concerning the execution of Gods decree.

The execution of Gods decree, is a most free, and iust worke of God: by which God doth in the determined time performe all things, which haue bene decreed frō euerlasting, and doth so performe them, as they were decreed.

For the workes of God are now in time so performed, that they do fully answere to his decree, that is to say, that those things which are decreed should all of them be done indeed, and as they were decreed, so they should be done.

The execution of Gods decree is two fold: either respecting this life or the life to come.

The execution of Gods decree, respecting this life, is that by which those workes are done, which God hath decreed to doe in this life.

Those workes are two fold. Creation and prouidence.

Creation, is a worke of God, by which he hath brought forth all creatures of nothing. Gene. 1.2.

A creature, is whatsoeuer hath bin made by God of nothing.

Now all the creatures of God were created very good. Therfore all nature as it is nature, is good, because it is the worke of God.

Of these creatures some are created according to the Image of God: some are not.

The Image of God, is that dignitie, and excellencie, in which the reasonable creatures, being created like vnto God, do excell other creatures.

Of this Image of God there are two parts, perfect reason, and perfect blessednesse.

Perfect reason, is a part of Gods Image, by which the reasonable creature, doth more expresly carie the Image of God his creatour, whilest by a certaine diuine force it knoweth plainlie things, without errour, as they are, and doth will and chuse no other thing, then that which doth please God.

And that perfect reason consisteth, both in the minde and in the will.

Perfect reason in the minde, is an excellent vnderstanding, rightly knowing all simple, particular, and generall things, which a created nature can know, and ioyning them together, or diuiding them, or reasoning by compared things, it hauing also by nature, some ingraffed & naturall knowledge, such as are the principles of arts, and rule of life, and a respectiue motion iudging of the proper actes thereof.

In the will there is both the conformitie of the will with God, and also free will.

The conformitie of the will with God, is that obedience, which the will doth vprighly performe to God, so that all inclinations, desires, and actions do agree with Gods will.

The free will of a reasonable creature, is the power of the will, chusing or refusing freely and of it owne proper motion, without compulsion, that which vnderstāding sheweth to be chosen or refused.

Thus farre concerning perfect reason: now concerning perfect blessednesse.

Perfect blessednesse is that other part of the image of God, by which a naturall creature, through an excellent ioy, taking pleasure in God alone, doth enioy perfect felicitie.

The creatures made according to the image of God, are Angels, and men. Angels, are created, vnderstanding, and inuisible spirites, neither susteined in any other (excepting in God alone) neither part of another.

And Angels are either good or euill.

Good Angels, are Angels which haue stood in their integritie in which they were made.

Their free will, is to good things onely, because they are already so confirmed in goodnesse, that their mind cannot be deceiued, nor erre in iudging, that is to say, in approuing, & misliking the obiect, neither can the will desire any other thing, thē that which the mind iudgeth, but chuse that which it approueth, refuse and reiect that which it misliketh. Iob. 4.18. Mat. 22.30. 1. Tim. 5.21. Ephes. 1.10. Col. 1.20.

The dutie of good Angels is two fold: either towardes God, or men.

Their dutie towards God is of two sorts: the first to do Gods will. Psal. 103.20.

The second to set forth God by continuall prayses. Psal. 103.20. and 148.2.

The dutie of Angels towardes men, is also two fold.

The one, to be a defence to the elect against all dangers, and against the subtleties and assaults of the enemies, and to cary the soules of the elect being dead, into the place of the blessed. Or else to minister to those that feare God in all their wayes. Heb. 1.14. Psal. 34.8. & 103.21. Mat. 18.10. Psal. 91.11. Dan. 10. and 12. Luke. 16.22.

Their other dutie is, to punish the euill. For the good Angels, are not onely the disposers of the goodnesse of God, but also sometime executers of punishment. 2. King. 29.35.

Hitherto concerning good Angels: now concerning euill Angels.

Euill Angels, are Angels who haue fallen from God. Iohn. 8.44. 2. Pet. 2.4. Epistle of Iude. 5.6. Ephes. 2.2.

The same are called deuils.

And they are the first authors of all sins, & do endeuour to seduce men by their temptations, and to stirre them vp to sin, as also by all meanes to turne them away from God, & to thrust them headlong into destruction.

The temptations of the deuill, are perswasions, sollicitings, and sturrings vp, by which he doth endeuour to draw men into sinne and destruction. After this manner he tempted our first parents. Genes. 3.1. So the deuill tempting Christ, sollicited him to distrust concerning Gods prouidence, as though God could not sustaine, and preserue him without bread. Mat. 4.3. he tempted him to rashnesse, and vnaduised boldnesse, that for the obtaining of glory, he might expose himselfe to vnnecessary daungers. vers. 6. he sollicited him to idolatry. vers. 8.

In euill Angels, we must consider both their office, and restraint.

If we respect their office, they are compelled to serue, and obey God in those workes, which it pleaseth God to performe by them.

Of this office there are two parts: For they are ordained both to afflict the godly, that their constancy might be proued. Iob. 1.12. and 2.6.7. 2. Corin. 22.7. as also to vexe the wicked, as officers, and tormentours appointed by God.

The restraint of the euill Angels, is the bounding, and limiting of their power and fury, that they are able to do no more, then God doth suffer them to do.

Their free will is to euill things onely. For seeing they are cast away from God for euer, & are hardened in euill, they can do nothing, nor hereafter shall do any thing but sin, that is to say, onely to approue with their minde, and chuse with their will, those things which are euill, and displease God, and therefore they shall suffer euerlasting punishment. Iohn. 8.44. 1. Iohn. 3.8. Mat. 3.8. Mat. 25.41. Iude. vers. 6. Reuel. 20.10.

Hitherto concerning Angels: now concerning man.

Man is a creature of God, made according to his Image, consisting of a body, and a reasonable soule.

We ought especially to consider, both his estate, and also his will.

The estate of a man is to be considered two wayes: one before the fall, another after the fall.

The estate of man before the fall, was that happy estate of his first integrity, in which man was made at the beginning. It is also called an vpright estate, or the estate of integrity or innocency.

The estate of man after the fall, is that estate into which all men fell afterward.

And that estate is two fold: corrupted, or renued.

The corrupt estate, is that vnhappy estate, which all men descending by carnall generation, haue fallen into through sinne.

The renued estate, is that estate of man, in which man is renued againe according to the Image of God.

And that renued estate is two fold: the one begū, the other perfected: the former is in this life, the other the life to come.

Hitherto concerning the state of man: now concerning his will.

The will of man, is that power of his will, chusing, or refusing that, which the vnderstāding sheweth to be chosen or refused.

And that was of one sort before the fall, and of another since the fall.

The will of man before the fall, was free in all things, because it could incline to either part, that is to say, to good or euill, so that it might chuse either the one or the other, yea & that so farre, that man by his own strength was able to stand or to fall.

For although man were so made, that he was good, and could know God aright, and performe to him right & perfect obedience, by the free motion of his owne will yet notwithstanding he was changeably good, that is to say, he was not so cōfirmed in the knowledge and obedience of God, but that a shew of some good being set before him, he might be inclined to fall away, and indeed did fall away of his owne proper motion.

<u>Thus much concerning the will of man before the fall.</u>

The will of man after the fall, is to be considered two wayes: first as it is in this life, secondly as it shalbe in the life to come.

In this life it is two fold: the one in the corrupted, or vnregenerated men, the other in the regenerated men.

In men corrupted or vnregenerated, the will is both bound and free.

Their will is free onely to euill, in all things, both in spirituall, and also in ciuill & outward matters. But freedome of the will to goodnesse, is lost through sinne.

True it is indeed, that the will of the vnregenerate, worketh freely, yet it can doe nothing but sinne. And sin doth always flow from this fountaine of the free will of man.

And although the vnregenerated sometimes doe performe some good workes morally, and such as of themselues are good, yet by accident they are become sinnes: because they do them not, by the true knowledge of God, & by faith, lastly because they erre from the true end, whilest they do not regard this, namely the honour of God. Heb. 11.6. Mat. 23.27.28. Rom. 1.18. and 14.23.

But the will of the vnregenerate is bound & captiue as concerning good & holy things, and specially concerning things belonging to saluation and eternall life. For the vnregenerate, cannot by their owne strength turne themselues to God, nor receiue the grace that God offereth them, nor vndertake or performe any worke pleasing God. Gen. 6.5. and 8.21. Iere. 13.10 23. & 17.9. Psal. 14.1.3. Rom. 3.10.11.12. Mat. 7.18. & 12.34. Ioh. 3.3. & 6.44. & 12.39. Rom. 7.18. and 7.7. 2. Cor. 3.5.

Hitherto concerning the will of man being corrupted: now concerning the will of the regenerated man.

The will of the regenerated man, is free, partly to good, partly to euill.

The will of the regenerated man to good is free by the speciall blessing & assistance of the holy spirit, who doth begin, continue, and make perfect in him his cōuersion to God & good works: & that so, that both the beginning, proceeding, and finishing of this cōuersion is the free gift of God: notwithstanding in the meane while the regenerated man is not idle, but worketh, being sturred vp by the holy spirit. Deut. 30.6. 1. Kin. 8.58. Iere. 31.33. Ezech. 11.19. and 30.26. Luke. 24.45. Ioh. 6.45. Actes. 16.14 Rom 6.18.2. Cor. 3.5. and 17. and 46. Phil. 1.6. & 2.13. Ephes. 4.24. Col. 3.20.

Againe the will of the regenerate man is free to euill first because the regeneration, & renewing of nature, that is to say, of the mind, will, & affections is onely begun, & not perfected in this life, and always the reliques of flesh or sinne doe remaine, which do somewhat both darkē knowledge in the minde, & also tosse & turne the will, so that we cannot by and by doe those things which we would. Mar. 9.24. Ro. 7.18. & so following. 1. Cor. 13.12

Secondly, because the regenerate are not always powerfully ruled by the holy spirit, but now & then for a time are as it were forsaken, and left to themselues by God (who doth not so manifest his power in thē as before time) that they falling into sin might be humbled. 2. Sam. 24.1. 1. King. 8.57. Psal. 51.13. Esa. 62.17. Eze. 16.6. & 63. Rom. 11.32. 2. Cor. 12.7.

Hitherto concerning the will of men in this life: now concerning their will in the life to come.

In the life to come there shalbe one will of those that are blessed, and another of those that are damned.

The will of the blessed after this life, shalbe free onely to good, & not to euill, so that they shall not onely not sin, nor chuse the euill, but they shall not be able to sinne, or to chuse the euill, that is to say, that they shall will nothing but that which is good.

And hereof there are two reasons.
- 1 Because their regeneration shalbe perfect, and not begun onely, as now it is. Mat. 22.30. 1. Cor. 3.12 .1. Iohn. 3.2.
- 2 Because they shall neuer be forsaken, but shalbe gouerned continually, & ruled powerfully of God in all their actions, that they should not erre frō a right course. 1. Cor. 15.28.

The will of the dāned shalbe onely to euill for euermore: because they shall alwayes be without any repentance, and hope of pardon & deliuerance, & shall remaine in the kingdome of Sathan, & be thrust forward by him and their owne lustes, and shall fight against God. Mat. 25.46. Mar. 9.43.

Hitherto concerning creation: now concerning the prouidence of God.

The prouidence of God, is a worke of God, by which he gouerneth all things according to his own will, & doth direct them to his owne glory, and to the saluation of the elect. Otherwise it is called the gouernement, the rule also, and kingdome of God. Psal. 93.1. and 97.1. and 99.1. and 103.19.

And that is a perpetuall testimony of Gods presence in all places.

Neither doth any thing happen rashly, or by chance, but all things are done by the prouidence of God, according to his fatherly counsell and will.

Neither yet is that done without Gods will, which is done contrary to his will.

Both good and euill is gouerned by the prouidence of God.

Good is that which God alloweth, as for example, all the substances of things, & their quantities and qualities, which they haue by creation, their motions, and changes, their actions and euents as farre forth as they are motions, and do agree with Gods nature and will, as it is expressed in his word.

Whatsoeuer therefore is remaining either in deuils or in men by creation, is good.

Good is either naturall, or morall.

Naturall good, is euery good thing which God hath created in nature, to those vses of men which please God, as the sunne, moone, the earth, the water, meat, drinke & rayment.

Morall good, is an action agreeing with the eternall, and vnchangeable wisedome of God, manifested in Gods law, which both by creation is ingraffed in the mindes of men, and afterwardes published abroad by Gods voyce. Or else morall good, is euery good action agreeing with the will of God reuealed in his word.

Thus much concerning good: now concerning euill.

Euill, is a destruction of the nature created by God.

And that is, either the euill of the offence, or of the punishment.

Both these euils are set downe. Iere. 18.8. If this nation shall turne away from their euill, concerning which I haue spoken against them, it shall also repent me of the euil which I purposed to haue done vnto it.

Euill of the offence■ is sinne.

Sinne, is euery thing contrary to the law of God.

Sinne is either of deuils or of men.

The sinne of the deuils is that, into which euill Angels haue fallen.

And that is two fold, their fall, & the malice following their fall.

The fall of the deuils, is their falling away from God, whereby they haue left their own standing, assigned them in heauen for ministration.

The malice following vpon the fall of the deuils, is that, whereby they are for euer made the enemies of God, and of men, and are caried with an vnreconcilable hatred towardes God, and men. 1. Iohn. 3.8.9. 1. Pet. 5.8. Ephes. 6.12.

Thus farre concerning the sinnes of deuils: now concerning the sinnes of men.

The sinne of men, is that sinne into which men haue fallen.

And that is of two sortes, either the sin of our first parents, or of their posterity.

The sinne of our first parents, is the sinne of Adam and Heuah.

And that is two fold: both the fall, and the corruption following the fall.

The fall of our first parents, is the eating of the forbidden fruite, by the persuasion and subtlety of the deuill, through which eating they did breake the commandement of God, and haue cast themselues and their posterity headlong into eternall death.

Now our first parents fell, both willingly, and by Gods prouidence.

That they fell willingly, it appeareth hereby, because they were endued with a will of their owne, which was free, and could not be compelled.

Thereupon it came to passe, that a shew of good, that is to say, of obtaining a diuine nature being set before them, they did fall, and sinne, the minde approuing that which was set before it, & the will inclining it selfe to embrace the same.

That they fell by Gods prouidence, it appeareth in the Prou. 16.4. Rom. 11.32. Gal. 3.

The corruption following the fall, is a darkening of the Image of God, by which there ceaseth to be in the mind the true, & perfect knowledge of God, in the will the freedome of choise to goodnesse, and in the hart the true loue & feare of God & a purpose, & desire to obey God, & there succeeded in the minde ignorance, and doubtfulnesse: in the wil, and hart stubburnnesse against God, and a froward disposition.

Thus much concerning the sinne of our first parents.

The sin of the posterity, is that into which all the posterity of Adam, & Heuah did fall. And that is two fold: originall or actuall sin.

Originall sin, is that sin, in which all of vs are conceiued, & borne, who do descend by a carnall generation. Paule calleth it the sinne dwelling in vs. Rom. 7.20. Psal. 51.7. Ephes. 2.3. Rom. 5.12.

The partes thereof are two: Originall guilt, and originall naughtinesse.

Originall guilt, is a naturall offence, & subiection to punishment, because of the fall of our first parents. Rom. 5.12. So death went ouer all men.

Originall naughtinesse, is a naturall deprauing and corruption of mans whole nature.

This naughtinesse is not the very nature of mā it selfe, but onely sticketh to mans nature, from which it is alwayes to be discerned, euen after the deprauing.

And that is both in the soule & in the body.

Naughtinesse in the soule is two fold: the darknesse of the minde, and the losse of free will, or of free choise to good, and the disorder of the affections of the hart, naughty disposition to vices.

Naughtinesse of the body is also two fold: the disorder of the moueable members, and diseases which come by nature.

Thus much concerning originall sinne: now concerning Actuall sinne.

Actuall sinne, is that sinne, which we our selues commit.

[1] And first, that is either inward, or outward.

Inward sinne, is euery euill thought, and doubting concerning God and his will, incredulitie and the rest.

Outward sinne, is euery word, deed, or gesture contrary to the law and will of God.

Outward sinne, is either hid or manifest.

An hid sinne, is that which no man is priuie of, besides he which did commit it.

A manifest sinne, is that sinne, which other men also are priuie vnto, and are offended, & made worse thereby. Therefore it is specially called an offence.

An offence is a speech or deed whereby an other is made worse.

An offence, is either giuen, or taken.

An offence giuen, is an vngodly doctrine, or euill example of maners, which doth hurt others, either because they doe imitate the same, or because by it men are discouraged from the Gospell.

An offence taken, is when either by some right doctrine, or necessary deed, hypocrites are offended, and conceiue hatred of the Gospell, and godly men. And that is also called a Pharisaicall offence.

[2] Againe sinne is either raigning, or not raigning: which some men call deadly or veniall.

A sinne raigning, is that sinne, which the sinner doth not resist by the grace of the holy spirit, regenerating him to eternall life, and therefore it maketh him subiect to eternall death, except he repent, and obtaine pardon by Christ.

A sinne not raigning, is that sinne which the sinner resisteth by the grace of the holy spirit, regenerating him to eternall life, and therefore he is not subiect to eternall death, because he repenteth him, and doth obtaine pardon by Christ.

Euery sinne in it owne nature, is deadly, that is to say, it deserueth eternall death, but it is made veniall, that is to say, it doth deserue pardon and forgiuenesse, so that it doth not bring to the regenerate death eternall, by grace through Christ.

[3] Moreouer, euery sin is either against conscience, or not against conscience.

Sinne against conscience, is a sinne when a man knowing the will of God, doth contrary to it of set purpose.

Sin which is not against conscience, is that sin, which is cōmitted of him, that knoweth not the will of God, or else the sin is acknowledged, and lamented of the sinner, to be a sin, yet it cānot perfectly in this life be auoyded: as for example, originall sin, and many other sinnes of ignorance and infirmity.

[4] Furthermore, sinne is either pardonable or vnpardonable.

Pardonable sin, is that sinne which is forgiuen to him that repenteth, and to him that asketh remission through Christ.

Such are all sinnes, except the sin against the holy Ghost.

Vnpardonable sinne, is that sinne which is not forgiuen, neither in this world, nor in the world to come. Mat. 12.31. Mar. 3.28. Luk. 12.10. Heb. 6.4.5.6. 1. Iohn. 5.16.

Of this sort, is the sinne against the holy Ghost.

The sinne against the holy Ghost, is that sin, where Gods truth is resisted, or denyed of set purpose, after that the minde is confirmed, and taught in the truth, by the testimony of the holy spirite, whosoeuer commit this sinne are punished by God with blindnesse, so that they can neuer repent, and therefore cannot obtaine forgiuenesse.

[5] Moreouer sinne is either affected, or vnaduised.

An affected sinne, is that sin which is committed of meere malice or stubburnnesse.

An aduised sinne, is that sinne which is cōmitted of rashnesse or infirmity.

[6] Lastly, euery sin is by it selfe, or by accidēt.

Sinnes by them selues, are all sins which are forbidden by the law of God.

Sinnes by accident, are the actions of the vnregenerate, which indeed are commanded by God, but yet they displease God, because of the defectes and vices concurring in the wicked: or else indifferent actions which are done with offence.

Thus farre concerning the euill of the offence: now concerning the euill of the punishment.

The euill of the punishment, is euery destructiō, or afflictiō, or forsaking of the reasonable creature whereby God punisheth sins.

Thus much concerning the subiect of Gods prouidence: now concerning the parts thereof.

Of the prouidence of God there are two parts: Action, and permission.

Augustine in his booke called Enchirideon to Laurentius. There is not any thing done, but that which the almighty would haue to be done, either suffering it to be done, or he him selfe doing it (and now nothing could be done, if he did not suffer it, neither doth he suffer any thing to be done against his will but willingly.) Nothing therfore is done but that which either God him selfe doth, or suffereth to be done.

The action respecteth good things which God himselfe doth, amongst which are numbred the euill of the punishments (as men call them) because they tend to that which is good morally.

The action of God is either by meanes or without meanes.

The action by meanes, is when God for the performing of certaine workes vseth the ministery of secōdary causes as instruments.

And the instruments which God vseth are either good or euill.

God doth alwayes vse well both of them, that is to say, both the good, and the euill instruments also.

God vseth the euill, either to exercise and try the faith, patience, and constancy of the elect, as it is manifest by the example of Iob: or else to chasten the elect: so doubtlesse Absalom was vsed by God to chasten Dauid: or to punish euill men, that the euill might be punished by the euill. Esay. 21.2.

Now although he vse euill instruments, yet he is not the author or partaker of any sin at all: which appeareth euen by this, that at the length he doth most seuerely punish those wicked instruments whose helpe he vsed. Esa. 14.5.6.29.

Although also euill men do nothing neither can doe any thing, but that which is decreed of God: yet they cannot be excused, neither can they haue any excuse, & then are worthily punished, because they doe not regard the decree and glory of God, neither that end which God hath purposed with himselfe: but their owne euill purpose, that they might bring that to effect, that is to say, that they may do those things which their natural malice doth suggest vnto thē, they being filled, with anger, enuy, harred, desire of reuenge & set no other end before them, but that they might satisfie their own desire, couetousnes, and ambitiō, that they might preserue or encrease their own estate, that they might ouerthrow the good, and that they might reuenge thēselues. Hereof there is a notable example, Esa. 50.5.6. and so forward. Esa. 14.5. and 5.7.6.

For the wicked do always set before them selues an euill end. Gene. 50.20.

Now though God moue and stirre vp the euill, that he might doe some good thing by thē: they notwithstanding moue themselues with a contrary motion, to do wickedly, and that they might will that which is euill, and performe the same also.

Yet in the meane while, God doth direct those euill things which the vngodly do, to a good end, namely to his owne glory, and the saluation of the elect.

For God knew that it did rather pertaine to his most omnipotēt goodnesse to turne euil to good, thē to suffer euill not to be at all.

Wherfore in that Sathan, and the wicked sin, it is of themselues, that they in sinning do this or that, it is by the power of God, that is to say, in that the euill are moued and doe worke, it is by the power of God, but that they worke euilly, that is to say, are moued and worke, with euill affections, euill counsels, in euill manner, and with an euill end, that is of themselues: for naughtinesse is to be distinguished from the action it selfe, with which the naughtinesse is adioyned.

Euery action, as it is an action, is of God: for in him we liue, we moue, and haue our being. Acts. 17.28. and he performeth all things by the counsell of his will. Ephes. 1.11. but the naughtinesse of the action, doth arise from the will of man, neither doth it touch God, who can so vse euill and wicked instruments, that in the meane space, he is not so much as once touched with any infection of euill.

What sin soeuer therefore is in the action, it doth cleaue vnto the instruments, by whom although those things are done, which God would haue to be done, yet they are not always done after that manner which pleaseth him: & they set before thēselues another end then that which God respecteth.

Both these kindes of instruments, to wit, both good and euill, are either ordinary or extraordinary.

Ordinary instruments, are those instruments which God vseth ordinarily to execute his decree.

Extraordinary are those which are contrary to the former.

Againe instruments, are either liuing or without life.

Liuing instruments, are either reasonable or voyde of reason.

Reasonable instruments, as for example Angels. 2. King. 6.17. Iob. 2.7. And men. Genesis. 45.4. 2. Sam. 16.10. Ierem. 25.9. Ezech. 21.21. Iohn. 19.11. Actes. 2.23. and 4.27.

Instruments voyde of reason: as for example, beastes. 2. Pet. 2.16. Ezech. 14.2. King. 2.24. Gene. 8.2. Exod. 8.2.

Instruments without life are these: brimstone, fire. Genesis. 19.24. Hayle. Exod. 9.22. Manna. Exodus. 16.4. flesh. Exodus. 16.13. meate and drinke. 1. Kings. 14.4. also drought, famine, disease, pestilence, the sword, warre, death. Esay. 13.4.17. For all these are the ministers of God.

Thus far cōcerning Gods action done by meanes: now concerning Gods action without meanes.

The actiō of God done without meanes, is that whereby God doth performe without meanes or instruments, whatsoeuer he will. Gene. 20.3. Mat. 4.4. Deut. 8.3. So Gene. 2.5. When as yet the Lord had not rayned on the earth, neither was there any man to till the ground, yet all things were greene, and florished in the field, and there were fruites in the fields.

Hereby we learne that God can euē without meanes, performe and bring foorth all things.

Neither yet doth it follow thereupon that the earth is not to be tilled, because God without meanes can bring forth of the earth all things, that is to say, although it rayne not, although the earth be not tilled. Because God afterward ordained meanes by which he would worke. Now we must vse these meanes or else we should tempt God.

Yea God would haue man to labour euen in the state of his integrity, namely that he might till and dresse the garden Eden. Gene. 2.15.

Thus farre concerning the action of God: now concerning his permission.

Gods permission, is the worke of Gods prouidence, whereby God according to his eternall decree permitteth the euill of the offence, or sin to be done, whilest he doth withdraw his grace from sinners, and doth not incline or bend their will to obey Gods will. Esa. 2.6. Actes. 14.16. Rom. 1.24.28. Psal. 81.13.

Permission is a suffering of the euils of the offence, that is to say, of sinnes which are not done by God himselfe, but he doth suffer thē to be done according to his decree. Esa. 2.6. Actes. 14.16. Rom. 1.24.

But God suffereth the euill the offence, so that it cānot be done except he be willing to it, & it cā no other wise be done thē he suffereth, nor no further then he permitteth, that he also may direct it to a good end.

He suffereth the Saints to fall into sin, that they being chastened for their sinne, he might bring them to the true knowledge of them selues, and to humility, Psal. 119.

It is good for me, ô Lord, that thou hast humbled me, that I might learne thy statutes.

He suffereth also the reprobate to fall into sinne, that he might shew the glory of his iustice in punishing them for their sin. Rom. 9.17. Exod 9.16.

For God would not being good, suffer any thing to be done euilly, except also he being omnipotent, could turne euill to good.

He hath not therefore by his eternall, immutable, most wise and most iust purpose at any time wrought or approued euill, but permitted onely, that the chiefe creatures should fall into sinne.

Howbeit the deuill and the wicked, yea all creatures are so in Gods power, that without his will, they cannot onely not do any thing, but they cannot so much as once moue them selues. Gene. 20.6. So the false Prophet Balaā could not curse the people of Israell. Num. 22. Iob. 1.12. Prouerb. 21.1. Actes. 17.25.28.

Hereupon we may gather two doctrines.

The first pertaineth to our cōfort, namely, that no euill can befall vs from the deuill or from wicked men, without the will and permission of God.

The other pertaineth to our instruction, namely, that whatsoeuer aduersity commeth to vs, our minde must be turned away from our enemies, and the euill men who hate vs, and be lifted vp to God, and we must beare all things patiently. Iob. 1. we must acknowledge the iudgements of God to be iust, and reuerence them. Psal. 119. It is good for me, ô Lord, that thou hast humbled me and so foorth. And we must commit our iniury to God, and so forth.

<u>Hitherto concerning the parts of Gods prouidence: the sorts follow.</u>

The prouidence of God is two fold: Generall or speciall.

The generall prouidēce of God, is that wherby the whole world is gouerned. Gen. 7.1, 2.3.

And that is declared, & especially beheld in the preseruation or destruction of things.

The preseruatiō of things, is that whereby God preserueth all creatures, the better to declare his loue towards them. Psal. 36.8.9. Psal. 104. throughout. 105.106. Mat. 6.26.30.

Preseruation is either vniuersall or speciall.

The vniuersall preseruation, is that whereby he is present with all and euery creature, euen with the euill, so that he may preserue them onely as long as pleaseth him. Psal. 104. throughout. Mat. 6.26.30.

That is made manifest by their succeeding one another, or by their continuance.

By their succeeding one another, whereby one sort dying or perishing another sort cōmeth in their roome: as for example, men after men, beastes, after beastes, corne after corne: or one season after another season, as for example the spring, after the winter, the sommer, after the spring, the fall of the leafe after sommer, winter after the fall of the leafe.

By their continuaunce, as for example, of those things which are voyde of these changes, as the continuance of the heauenly motions, of the sunne, and other starres, of the continuall springing of riuers, &c.

Particular preseruatiō, is that whereby he doth take the care of euery particular thing seuerally. Mat. 6.30. and 10.29.30. Psal. 56.9. God nūbreth euen the teares of his children.

The destruction of things, is that whereby God doth destroy whatsoeuer he will, that he might shew euident examples, of his most iust iudgements. Psal. 104.29. and Psal. 105. & 10. Gene. 7.4. and 19.24. Num. 16.31.

The vse of this doctrine of Gods prouidence is three fold.

- 1. That we should be patient in aduersities. Rom. 5.3. Iam. 1.3. Iob. 1.21.
- 2 That we should be thankefull in prosperitie. Deut. 8.10. 1. Thess. 3.•8.
- 3 That we should haue a most sure hope layed vp for the time to come, in God our most faithfull father, certainly knowing that there is nothing that can draw vs away from his loue. Rom 5.2.4.5.6. Rom. 8.38.39.

<u>Hitherto concerning the generall prouidence of God: his speciall prouidence followeth.</u>

The speciall prouidence of God, is that prouidence whereby God doth particularly gouerne men.

The workes of Gods speciall prouidence, are either vniuersall, or particular.

The vniuersall workes, are those which belong to all men generally.

And the vniuersall workes are these, predestination, the naturall manifestation, and affliction, the hid motion of the wils of men, and the gouerning of all humane actions.

Predestination is an ordaining of men being fallen either to eternall life, or to eternall death.

Predestination is two fold: Election or reprobation.

Election and reprobation are properly referred to mankind, already made & fallen, & corrupted by sinne: but by a metonymie or putting of the effect for the cause, euen the very decree of chusing and reiecting is called by that name also.

Election is that predestination, whereby God of his free mercy doth deliuer out of the common destruction, whomsoeuer it pleaseth him. Ephes. 2.3.4.5.6.7.

God is pleased to declare his mercy on the elect: because when he might most iustly cast away all mankind for sinne, into which they had fallē willingly, for we all were the sonnes of wrath by nature, euen as well as others: he of his free mercy deliuered some from that cōmon destruction, that euery mouth might be stopped, and the whole glory of our saluation might be attributed to God alone. Ephe. 2.3.4.5.6.7.

Reprobation, is that predestination by which God according to his iustice, doth leaue those, on whom he will not take mercy, in the destruction into which they haue willingly throwen themselues headlong.

<u>Hitherto concerning predestination: now concerning the naturall manifestation of God.</u>

The naturall manifestation of God, is that which is done by the helpe of nature, to this end, that the excuse of the ignorance of God, & of sin, might be taken away from all men.

And that naturall manifestation is either by the law of nature, or by the workes of nature.

The law of nature, is a naturall knowledge ingrauē in the harts of men in the first creation, teaching a difference betweene honest and dishonest things, that we may seeke after the first & eschew the latter. Rom. 1.32. & 2.15.

The manifestation of God, by the workes of nature, is that naturall manifestation, by which through the workes of creation God doth shew forth his eternall power and diuinity. Rom. 1.19.20.

<u>Hitherto concerning the naturall manifestation of God: now concerning afflaction.</u>

Affliction, is a worke of Gods speciall prouidence, whereby God according to his eternall decree doth afflict men.

Affliction, is either the punishment or the crosse.

Punishment, is an affliction, which God layeth on men for sinne.

And that is either Gods chastisement, or his reuengement.

Chastismēt is a punishmēt, whereby God chasteneth the elect for their sinnes, that he might sturre them vp to repentance. Esay. 2.17. Psal. 119.71.

Gods reuengement is that punishment, whereby God doth take vēgeance on the sins of the wicked, that he might destroy them.

Gods reuengement is two fold, spirituall or bodily.

Gods spirituall reuengement is that which doth pertaine to spirituall things or to the soule.

And that is either the hardening of thē, or the withdrawing of Gods grace.

The hardening of them, is a spirituall reuengement, when God by his iust iudgement doth leaue some in their naturall blindnesse, and naughtinesse

The withdrawing of Gods grace, is a spirituall reuengement, when God for the sins of men doth take away his grace, from them whom he had begun to enlighten.

The bodily reuengement, is a reuengemēt which God layeth on the wicked in things pertaining to the body.

Againe reuengement is either temporall or eternall.

The temporall reuengement is a punishmēt, which is layed on the wicked in this life, that by it as by a preparation, they might be prepared, to the most grieuous punishment of hell, which at the length remaineth for them.

Eternall reuengement, is a punishment which the wicked shall endure in hell for euermore without any end.

Hitherto concerning the punishment: now concerning the crosse.

The crosse is the afflictiō, both of the whole Church, & specially of the particular and holy members thereof, but not for their sin, but that the godly treading in the steps of the crosse of Christ, may be conformed to his Image. 1. Pet. 4.13.15. Phil. 3.10. Rom. 8.28. Coloss. 1.24. Heb. 12.2. 1. Pet. 2.21.

And this crosse is two fold, temptation & martyrdome.

The diuine temptation, is the crosse of the godly, by which God tryeth the faith which they haue in his promises, by present or imminent affliction, and setteth the same before all men to be beheld and imitated.

And that is either inward or outward.

Inward temptation is two fold, either the trouble of the minde, or the striuing betweene the spirit and the flesh, as it appeareth in the example of Abraham.

Outward temptation, as the affliction of the body, the losse of goods and children, & so sorth, as it is manifest in the example of Iob.

Martyrdome, is the crosse of the godly, which they for the truth of Christ suffer of the world.

And martyrdome is either to death, or not to death.

Martyrdome to death, is a shedding of the bloud and life, for a finall confirmation of the truth of God, as it were by an outward and vndoubted testimony. Iohn. 21.18.

Martyrdome not to death, is an enduring of slanders, reproches, prison, exile and other dangers for the truths sake. 2. Cor. 4.8. and 6.4.8. and 12.10.1. Pet. 4.14.

Thus farre concerning affliction: now concerning the secret mouing of the will.

The secret mouing of the will, is a worke of Gods speciall prouidence, when God boweth the wils of men hither and thither as pleaseth him. Prou. 23.1. Iob. 12.20.24.

For all the actions euen of euill men, which they in liuing do performe, are done and gouerned, although by the secret, yet by the good & iust will of God. All the ⟨...⟩ . I say euen of the wicked, so farre forth as they are actions, or motions to the things set before them, or as they are punishments or chastisements, or the executions of gods will, all all these, I say, God doth powerfully will and rule. Gene. 45.5.7.8. Exod. 7.3. and 10.1. Deut. 2.30. Ios. 11.19.20. Iudg. 3.1.12. 2. Sam 12.11.12.2. Sam. 16.10.11.2. Sam. 24.1.1. King. 22.19.20.21.22.23. Iob. 1.12.21. and 2.3.6. and 19.6. Psal. 107.40. Esay. 19.2.3. Iohn. 13.27. That which thou doest do quickly. Actes. 2.23. and 4.27. and 7.43. Rom. 1.24.28. Reuel. 17.17.

The secret motion of the wils, is either the softening, or the hardening of them.

The softening, is a secret motion, by which God boweth the wils of men, that they willingly doe that which is acceptable to God. So God cōmanded the widow, that is to say, by the secret force of his prouidēce hebowed her will, that she should willingly nourish Elijah.

The hardening is a secret motion, whereby God doth bow mēs will that they should not haue a will to do that which is acceptable to God. So God hardened Pharaoh that he should be vnwilling to let the people go, nor to make peace with them. So God hardened Shemei that he should not cease from cursing 2. Sam. 16.22.

<u>Thus farre concerning the secret motion of the will: now concerning the gouerning of all wo dly or humane actions.</u>

The gouerning of all humane actions is a worke of Gods speciall prouidence, whereby he doth always so gouerne all the actions of men, as pleaseth him.

The parts thereof are the direction of the actions, and the restraint of the wicked.

The direction of the actiōs is the worke of Gods speciall prouidēce, by which God doth so gouerne the actiōs of mē, that they should be able to do nothing, but that which he hath already decreed with himselfe, neither after any other sort thē that which he hath decreed, that he might also direct it to a good end. Rom. 9.17. and. 11.11.1. Cor. 11.19. Phil. 1.12.2. Thess. 2.11.12. Reuel. 17.17.

The restraint of the wicked, is the worke of Gods speciall prouidence, whereby God doth determine, and limit as it were the power of the wicked mē, that they should be able to do no more then God suffereth them.

<u>Hitherto concerning the generall workes of Gods speciall prouidence: the particular follow.</u>

The particular workes of Gods speciall prouidence, are those which doe pertaine to part of mankind.

Such are the supernaturall manifestation of Gods will, the working of miracles, the calling, the heauenly couenant, and the heauenly signe.

The supernaturall manifestation of Gods will, is the worke of Gods speciall prouidence, whereby after a speciall manner he manifesteth his will to men in the Church. Psal. 103.7. Heb. 1.1.2.

Of this there are two parts, the reuelation of doctrine, or the foretelling of things to come.

The reuelation of doctrine, is either of the doctrine of the law, or of the Gospell.

The law of God is a doctrine, which commaundeth vs what we must do, and what we must leaue vndone, requiring perfect obedience, both inward and outward towardes God, and promising eternall life to those that obey it: but threatning eternall punishments to those that breake any part thereof. Mat. 19.16.17.18.19. Mat. 7.12. Leuit. 18.5. Ezech. 10.11. Rom. 10.5. Gala. 3.10. Deut. 27.26. Iam. 2.10.

The law of God, is either generall or speciall.

The generall law of God, is that whereby all men generally, are alwayes bound, except God himselfe, doe specially command another thing: After this sort the ten cōmandements are generall.

For all generall lawes are to be vnderstood with this condition: to wit, Except God him selfe command another, as:

Thou shalt not make to thy self any grauē Image: namely except God doth especially command to make it, as when he commanded to make the Cherubins, and brasen Serpent: and so forth.

Thou shalt not steale, namely except God doth specially command, as when he commanded to spoyle the Egyptians. Thou shalt not kill, namely except God doth specially command, as when he commanded Abraham that he should sacrifice his sonne Isaack. Honour thy parēts, obey thy parents, namely except God command another thing thē our parents: For then we must not obey our parents but God.

The particular law of God, is that which he made specially to certaine men, in some certaine case.

Therfore it doth not ouerthrow the generall law of God: because the particular law, is not perpetuall, but for a certaine time, neither doth it belōg to all, but onely to those to whom it was made specially, neither is it of force in all cases, but onely in that which God himselfe hath by name expressed.

Againe the law of God, is either perpetuall, or for a certaine time.

The perpetuall law of God, is that law which doth alwayes bind all reasonable creatures to obedience: and that is called the morall law.

The morall law is that law which teacheth how euery one ought to behaue himselfe, in inward, and outward maners, that his whole life may be agreeable to Gods will.

The summe of that is comprehended in the decaloge or ten commandements.

The decaloge or ten commandements is a briefe summe of the morall law, containing ten preceptes.

And that is deuided into two tables or parts.

The first table containeth foure cōmandements, concerning our duties toward God, or concerning loue towardes God, or concerning his worship.

The first commandement is this: thou shalt no haue strange Gods before me.

In this commandement God forbiddeth to haue strange Gods before him.

A strange God, is euery thing, in which a man putteth his confidence besides the true God, or that which a man doth feare or loue more then God, or equally with God, or to which he giueth diuine worship contrary to the expresse word of God.

To haue strange Gods, is to put his confidence in any thing, which is not the true God, or to loue, or feare that more then God, or as well as God, or to giue to it diuine worship contrary to the expresse word of God.

Not to haue strange Gods before God, is to eschew all idolatry, not onely in the sight of men, but euen in the heart, because God seeth all things.

The second commandement is this: thou shalt not make to thy self any grauen image, neither shalt thou counterfeit any Image of those things, which are in heauen aboue, or in the earth beneath, or in the waters vnder the earth, thou shalt not bow downe to them, nor worship them. For I am the Lord thy God, strong, iealous, reuenging the sinnes of the fathers vpon the children, and that vnto the third and fourth generation of those that hate me: and shewing mercy vnto thousandes of them that loue me and keepe my commandements.

In this commandement God forbiddeth, both the framing of Images for Religions sake, and also the worshipping of them.

And by Image is vnderstood (by putting the part for the whole) euen all the worship of God deuised by men.

Therefore Images are not to be borne withall in Churches, which might be in steed of bookes to the ignorant people.

For neither doth it become vs to be more wise then God, who will haue his Church to be taught, not with dumbe Images, but with the liuely preaching of his word. Iere. 10.8. Haba. 2.18.19. Luke. 16.29. Neither is God to be otherwise worshipped thē he hath prescribed in his word.

Now there is a threatning and promise added to this commandement, that it might driue vs the more powerfully from Idolatry, as from an abhominable sinne.

In the threatning God nameth himselfe strong and iealous.

He calleth himselfe indeed, strong, that we might feare the power which he hath to reuenge.

He calleth himselfe iealous, because he neuer without punishmēt suffereth his honour to be giuen to any other.

But in the threatning God doth threaten punishments, both to the sinners themselues, and also to their posterity.

God for two causes threateneth punishments to the posterity of sinners.

- 1. That he might shew the greatnesse of sinne, which draweth punishments not onely vpon them that commit them, but vpon their posterity also, if God should deale according to the straightnesse of his iustice.
- 2. That at the least men fearing the punishment that shall light on their posterity, they might abstaine from sinne.

That the posteritie be punished for the sinnes of the parents, it is not against the iustice of God: for such is the naughtinesse of our nature, that except God regard vs in his singular mercy, we should all of vs perseuere in the sinnes of our parents.

Thus farre concerning the threatening.

In the promise ioyned to this commandement, God promiseth that he will blesse euen the posterity of the godly.
There are two causes leading him to this.
- 1. That he might expresse the greatnesse of his mercy toward the godly, whereby he doth blesse not onely them, but their porterity also.
- 2. That happynesse being promised to our posterity, he might sturre vs vp more earnestly to godlinesse.

And he saith, that he will blesse to the thousandth generation, & punish at the least to the fourth, that he might testifie, that he is not delighted with the destruction, but with the saluation of men: & that he doth not punish, but for the manifestation of his iustice.

Hitherto concerning the second commandement: now concerning the third.

The third cōmandement is this: thou shalt not vse the name, of the Lord thy God rashly. For the Lord thy God will not let him go vnpunished, who taketh his name in vaine.

In this commandement God forbiddeth the vaine vse of his name, and establisheth that prohibition with a grieuous punishmēt.

The vaine vsing of Gods name, is when any false or reprochfull thing is spoken of God, or when a man by lightnesse or vngodlinesse doth falsly or rashly sweare by God, or when one doth bitterly curse others, by custome or desire of reuengement.

The establishment of this commandement containeth a threatning of punishmēt, that God might shew, that the profanation of his name is to be accounted amongst most grieuous sinnes.

The fourth commandement is this: Remember that thou keepe holy the Sabaoth day. Six dayes shalt thou labour and doe all that thou hast to doe. But the seuenth day is the Sabaoth of the Lord thy God, in it thou shalt doe no manner of worke, thou nor thy sonne, nor thy daughter, thy manseruant, nor thy maidseruant, the cattell nor the stranger that is within thy gates. For in six dayes the Lord made heauen and earth, the sea and all that in them is, and rested the seuenth day, wherefore the Lord blessed the Sabaoth day, and hallowed it.

The sanctification of the Sabaoth day is the appointing of an holy day to the publike worship of God: or else it is to bestow a day in holy workes and exercises.

There are foure parts of the sanctification of the Sabaoth▪ the handling of Gods word, the vsing of the Sacraments publicke calling on God by prayer, and the exercising of the workes of mercy.

God for two causes would haue a certaine time appointed for the ministery of the Church.

- 1. For our weaknesse, who otherwise do seldome wholy giue our selues to the meditation of heauenly things.
- 2. That rest from labour might be giuen to those, who are vnder other mens authoritie.

Now we are not bound to the seuenth day: for Christ by his comming hath abolished the ceremonies of Moses.

Hitherto concerning the first table of the ten commandements: The second followeth.

The second table of the ten commandements, consisteth of sixe commandements concerning our duties or loue towardes our neighbours.

And those commandements are in order, the fift, the sixt, the seuenth, the eight, the ninth, and the tenth.

The fift commandement is this: Honour thy father and thy mother, that thy dayes may be prolonged in the land, which the Lord thy God shall giue thee.

Of this commandement there are two partes: In the first part God commandeth the performance of honour due to our parents.

By the name of parents are vnderstood not onely those who begat vs, but euen all superiours who are ouer vs, or who are set ouer vs by God to gouerne vs.

Now of the honour due to our superiours, there are fiue partes, reuerence, loue, obedience in all things not forbiddē by God, thankefulnesse, and patience in bearing their infirmities, and slips.

In the second part of this commandement, God promiseth long life to those that honour their parents, and that for two causes.

- 1. That he might shew what account he maketh of obedience to superiours.
- 2. That he might allure vs performe it.

The sixt commandement is this: thou shalt not kill.

In this commandement God forbiddeth man-slaughter.

By man-slaughter is vnderstood, not onely the outward hurt of our owne life, or of our neighbours, but euen euery cause of hurt and slaughter, as are anger, gestures expressing anger, iniurious facts, reproch, hatred, desire of priuate reuenge, and so forth.

The seuenth commandement is this: thou shalt not commit adultery.

Wherin God forbiddeth all vncleannesse of the mind or of the body, both in mariage, and out of mariage.

The eight commandement is this: thou shalt not steale.

Wherein God forbiddeth theft.

Theft is euery vniust translating or turning of any other mens goods to himselfe, whether it be done priuily or openly, or else whether it be done by violence, or deceipt, & shew of right. Or else theft, is euery manner of doing any thing forbidden by God.

Such as are these, pillage, taking away of other mens goods, an vniust weight, an vniust elle, an vnequall measure, deceiptfull ware, coūterfeit coine, vsury, couetousnes, the abusing of Gods gifts.

The ninth commandement is this: Thou shalt not beare false witnesse against thy neighbour.

Wherein God forbiddeth false witnesse, both in iudgement, and also out of iudgement.

Therefore by false witnesse, is vnderstood, euen periury, slander, backebiting, reproch, cursing, euill suspition, prating, flattering, lastly all sorts of lyes.

The tenth commandement is this: Thou shalt not couet thy neighbours house, thou shalt not couet thy neighbours wife, nor his manseruant, nor his maidseruant, nor his oxe, nor his asse, nor any thing that is thy neighbours.

Wherein God forbiddeth euen the least desire and thought contrary to Gods law.

For in the sight of God not onely the outward euill deed is sin, but euen the thought & consultation of committing an euill deed, although it be not brought to passe.

<u>Hitherto concerning the explication of the ten commandements: now concerning the vses of the morall law.</u>

The vses of the morall law are of two sorts: common or proper.

The common vses are those, which doe equally belong to the elect, and reprobate.

And they are three. 1. To preserue discipline, both in the regenerate, and vnregenerate, and that two wayes First, because it bindeth all men, that they should gouerne the moueable or outward members, to the intent that the outward deedes may agree with Gods law. Secondly, because it establisheth punishments euen bodily in this life, against those who commit outward offences, which punishments God doth execute on the guilty, either by the Magistrate, or by some other meanes.

2. To teach vs to know, what a one God is.

3. To teach vs to acknowledge our sinnes. Rom. 3▪ that the whole world might be guilty before God. By the law cōmeth the knowledge of sinne. Rom. 7.7.

The proper vses of the law are those which do belong to the elect onely, or to the reprobate onely.

The vses of the law pertaining particularly to the elect are these.

- 1. To stirre vp and increase repentance in the elect.
- 2. To kindle in the elect desire to seeke forgiuenesse of sinnes, and righteousnesse in Christ.
- 3. To stirre vp, and thrust forward the elect to an endeuour to the perpetuall meditation, and calling vpon the holy spirite for grace, whereby they may be renued daily, more and more, according to the image of God.
- 4. To stirre vp and increase in them the desire of perfection, which we shall obtaine in the life to come.
- 5. To be to the elect a direction how to liue, and a rule of good workes. For it teacheth what workes please God.

The vses of the law belonging onely to the reprobate are three.

- 1. To make them without excuse.
- 2. The more to harden them.
- 3. To prepare them to desperation.

Thus farre concerning Gods perpetuall law: now concerning the law of God for a certaine time.

The law of God for a certaine time, is that which was onely for a certaine time prescribed to the people of Israell, and is abrogated by the comming of the Messias.

And that law is either ceremoniall or iudiciall.

The ceremoniall law, is that law which gaue commaundement concerning ceremonies to be obserued in the publicke worship of God, which did scrue to instruct the people of Israell, of the manner of their eternall saluation, by Christ to come.

The iudiciall law, is a law, which giueth commaundement, concerning the politicke gouernement of the Iewes, that is to say, of the order and offices of Magistrates, iudgementes, punishments, contractes, of the distinguishing of gouernements, made for this end, that iustice, and publicke peace might be of force among Citizens, and the lawes of God might be deliuered from contempt.

<u>Hitherto concerning the law of God, now concerning the Gospell.</u>

The Gospell is that wholesome doctrine, concerning Christ, already shewed and manifested.

Christ, is the onely begotten sonne of God, made man for our saluation. Iohn. 1.14. 1. Iohn. 4.2. 1. Tim. 3.16.

Of the knowledge of Christ, there be two parts, the first concerning his person, the second concerning his office.

The person of Christ, is one, because Christ is one.

Of the knowledge of Christes person, there be two parts: the first concerning the natures in the person of Christ, the other concerning his state.

There are two natures in the person of Christ, the diuine, and the humane nature.

Therefore Iesus Christ is true God, and true man in one person. Rom. 1.3.4. and 9.5. 1. Iohn. 4.2. 1. Timot. 3.16. Coloss. 2.9. Heb. 2.14.16. Iohn. 1.1.

<u>Thus farre concerning the natures in the person of Christ: now concerning his state.</u>

The state of Christes person is two fold: his humiliation, or exaltation. Phil. 2.7.8.9. Luke. 24.26.

The humiliation of Christ is that state of his, in which he did abase himselfe below all creatures. Phil. 2.7.

Of his humiliation there are two partes? his incarnation, and obedience.

The incarnation of Christ, is part of the humiliation of the sonne of God, when taking the humane nature, he was manifested in the flesh. Iohn. 1.14. 1. Tim. 3.16.

The parts of the incarnation of Christ, are both his conception by the holy spirite, and the personall vnion of his two natures, and also his birth.

The conception of Christ by the holy spirite, is the forming of the humane nature of Christ, of the flesh and bloud of the virgine Mary, by the miraculous working of the holy spirit. Mat. 1.18.20. Luke. 1.31.35.

The personall vnion of the two natures in Christ, is such a coupling of them as they might be one person. 1. Tim. 3.16. Coloss. 2.9. Gal. 4.4. Heb. 2.16.

In this personall vnion, both the distinction of the two natures is to be considered, and also the effectes of the vnion.

In the personall vnion, the natures remaine distinct, and not confused, whether we respect their essence, or the properties, or operations. Rom. 1.3.4. and 9.5. 1. Tim. 9.16. Heb. 9.14. 1. Pet. 3.18. and 4.1.

As therefore in that one person of Christ there be two natures: so there is a double minde, or vnderstanding a double will, working, wisedome, strength, power, vertue, and so forth. The one heauenly and not created: the other humane, and created. Luke. 2.52. Mar. 11.13. and 13.32. 1. Iohn. 2.1.17. Iohn. 2.25. and 6.64. and 5.20. Heb. 1.9. Iohn. 1.33. and 4.6. Heb. 1.3. Iohn. 2.19. and 10.18.

And each of the natures retaineth and keepeth his owne essentiall properties, neither doth it communicate them, to the other nature, and that for two causes: the first is, least the natures should be mingled and confounded: the other, that there might foreuer remaine a difference betweene the natures. Luke. 24.39.

For he that confoundeth the properties, confoundeth the natures: and he that taketh away the properties, taketh away the natures.

Thus farre concerning the distinction of the natures in the personall vnion: now concerning the effects of the vnion.

The effectes of the vnion are two fold: the one, the exaltation of the nature, assumed to the highest and vnspeakeable dignitie, and the communicating of the Idioms, or proprieties.

The exaltation of the assumed nature to the highest and vnspeakeable dignitie, is that honour, which the person of the sonne of God hath communicated to the nature assumed, so that he hath exalted it aboue all Angels & men, whom he surpasseth, and excelleth by most farre and vnspeakeable degrees. Heb. 14. Mat. 28.18. Iohn. 17.2. Phil. 2.9. Ephes. 1.20.22.

That exaltation consisteth chiefly in these three points.

1. In the personall vnion with the word: because the humane nature is assumed into the vnitie of the person of Gods sonne: so that it is the proper flesh of the eternall son of God, Heb. 2.16.

2. In the giftes, because it hath the fulnesse of all the giftes of the holy spirite, which can be in a creature, that is to say, it hath not onely some giftes, as the rest of the Saints, who haue them according to measure: but all giftes, not onely in number, but euen in the most excellent degree. Iohn. 3.34.

Those giftes giuen to the humanitie of Christ, are created qualities: because his humanitie is crea·ed.

That truely is adorned with most excellent, and incomprehensible giftes, but such as doe not ouerthrow and destroy the same.

3. In the fellowship of the office, both of the mediatour betweene God and the beleeuers, and also of the head of the Church, and of the Iudge of the whole world. Mat. 28.18. Phil. 2.9. Ephesians. 1.20.22, Psal. 110.1.1. Timot. 2.5. 1. Iohn. 2.12. Heb. 7.25.26.27. and 8.1. and 9.24.

<u>Hitherto concerning the exaltation of the nature assumed: now concerning the communicating of the Idioms or properties.</u>

The communicating of the Idioms or properties, is a Sinecdoche, whereby that is spoken of Christs person, which is proper to one of the natures in the person. Iohn. 3.13. Actes. 20.28. 1. Cor. 2.8. 1. Iohn. 1.1. and 3.16.

For because of the personall vnion of the two natures, their properties are common to the person.

And the communicating of the Idioms or properties, haue a place in the concreet, or primitiue, but not in the Abstract or deriuatiue.

The Concreet, or primitiue, is a name vnderstood of the person of Christ, as these, God, Man, Christ, Iesus, the sonne of God, the sonne of man, and so forth.

The Abstract or deriuatiue, is a name vnderstood of one of the natures onely in the person of Christ, as these, the Godhead, the manhood, flesh. Iohn. 1.14. The seed of Abraham. Heb. 2.16.

And if in steed of the Abstract, the Cōcreet be sometime vsed, for the most part there is added a note or particle of difference restraining it to one or other of the natures: sometime also it is vttered absolutely, without any note of difference expressed, yet vnderstood.

The notes of difference are these, by, nigh to, as long as, or vntill, in, through, as much as, and those that are like these. Rom. 1.3.4. 1. Tim. 3.16. Heb. 9.14. 1. Pet. 3.18. and 4 1. Rom. 9.5. Actes. 2.30.

And by these notes of difference is signified the property of the one nature, which cā not be spoken of the other nature.

As therefore it is most rightly sayd of Christ, God is borne of the virgine, suffered vnder Pontius Pilate, crucified, dead and buried, and so forth.

So also it is most rightly sayd of the same Christ, he is a man eternall, present euery where, omnipotent, knowing all things.

Contrariwise, as this is a most wicked and blasphemous speech, to say, the Godhead is borne of the virgine, suffered vnder Pontius Pilate, crucified, dead, and buried: so this is a most wicked and blasphemous speech, to say, that the humanitie of Christ is eternall, present euery where, omnipotent, knowing all things.

Thus much concerning the personall vnion.

The natiuitie of Christ is that whereby he was borne of the virgine Mary at Bethlehē, that he might be our Sauiour. Luke. 2.4. Mat. 2.1.5.

Thus farre concerning the incarnation of Christ: now concerning his obedience.

The obedience of Christ, is the other part of his humiliatiō, whilest he was in all things obedient to his father. It is also called the righteousnesse of Christ. Esay. 53. Heb. 5.8. Although he were the sonne of God, yet he learned obedience by those things which he suffered.

Of the obedience of Christ there are two parts: the fulfilling of the law, and the paying of the punishment for our sinnes.

The fulfilling of the law, is the first part of Christes obedience, whereby in his whole life he performed for vs perfect obedience to the law of God.

Otherwise it is called the actiue righteousnesse of Christ, and also the obedience of the holy life of Christ.

The paying of the punishment for our sinnes, is the other part of Christes obedience, whilest he for vs sustained the punishment which we had deserued, that he might satisfie for vs the most seuere iustice of God: so that we are no more bound to suffer that punishment, seeing Christ hath payed it for vs. Otherwise it is called the passiue righteousnesse of Christ: or the obedience of his Passion and death.

The partes of paying the punishment for our sinnes, are both his Passion, and death, & also his burying and descending to hell.

The Passion of Christ, is that part of his obedience, when hee in body and soule sustained the wrath of God against sinne. Heb. 9.26.28. and 10.11. Dan. 9.24. Esay. 53.5.

The parts of the Passion of Christ, are, the suffering of manifold euils, euen presently from his birth, to the institution of the holy Supper: and that solemne and most grieuous Passion in the end of his life.

The manifold euils from his birth to the institution of the holy Supper, are either of the body, or of the soule.

The euils of the body were both pouerty & dangers of life: and also diuers infirmities.

He sustained pouertie, Mat. 8.20. and 21.1.2. and 27.55. Luke. 9.58. that he might enrich vs with heauenly gifts. 2. Cor. 8.9.

The manifold daungers of his life, were these, for which he was both led into exile, Matth. 2.14.15. and also he did often yeeld for a time to the furies of the enemies. Mar. 3.6.7. Iohn. 7.1. and 11.53.54.

The infirmities of the body, Heb. 5.2. were hunger, Mat. 4.2. and 21.18. and thirst, Ioh. 4.8. wearinesse. Iohn. 4.6. teares. Iohn. 11.35.

The euils of the soule, were both ignorance, and temptations: as also sadnesse, and ignominie.

For Christ knew not certaine things, vntill he knew them by feeling. Mat. 11.13. he knew not the day & houre of iudgement. Mar. 13.32.

His temptations, were the assaultes of the deuill and his ministers, by which they did endeuour to seduce him to sinne, Mat. 4.1. or else to confound him, and lay him open to reproch, Matth. 22.35. or to cast him into danger of life. Mat. 22.15.16.

But he was therfore tempted, that he might helpe those that are tēpted. Heb. 2.17.18. & 4.15. Also that he might teach vs by his example, how we ought to meet with, and resist the temptations of the deuill and his instruments.

His sadnesse, was that whereby his soule was heauy and troubled. Iohn. 12.27.

His ignominies were manifold, vniust accusations, and slanders. Mat. 12.24. Mar. 11.19. reproches, reuilings. Iohn. 8.48.

His base account, and neglect. Mar. 6.3.4. reiection, contempt, and that truely among his owne.

<u>Hitherto of the euils which Christ suffered from his birth, euen to the last, and solemne acte of his Passion.</u>

That last and solemne act of Christes Passion, comprehendeth both his striuing in the garden, and his betraying, as also his iudgement.

The striuing of Christ in the garden, was that whereby he did terribly striue with the most vehement feeling of Gods horrible wrath against sinne, and with the horrour of Gods curse. Mat. 26.37. & so forward. Out of which he at the length scaping conquerour, he brought so to passe that death should no more be fearefull vnto vs.

The parts of his striuing, are both the feare, and trouble of the soule.

The feare of Christ, was that he feared more and more, that horrour hanging ouer him. Heb. 5.7.

The trouble of his soule, was the sadnesse of his soule, whereby it was most grieuously touched with sorrow, anguish and griefe Mat. 26.37.38.

The effectes of his striuing, were his affectionate and earnest prayer, and his sweating of bloud.

The affectionate and earnest prayer of Christ, was that whereby he asked of his father, the taking away of that horrour. Matth. 26.39.42.44.

Christes sweating of bloud, was when sweat, as it were drops of bloud, did fall on the earth. Luke. 22.44.

Thus farre concerning the striuing of Christ: now concerning his betraying.

His betraying was this, whereby Iudas Iscariot, that vnfaithfull disciple, receiuing thirty peeces of siluer for an hire, deliuered Christ to the Princes of the Priestes, and to the elders of the people of the Iewes. Matth. 26.47. and so forward.

Thus much concerning the betraying of Christ.

Christ was drawen into two sorts of iudgement, to the iudgement of the Priest and of the ciuill magistrate.

In the former, false witnesses being, produced in vaine, he was at length by Cayphas slandered, and condemned for blasphemy. Mat. 26.57. and so forward.

The ciuill iudgemēt is two fold, the one before Pilate, the other before Herod, by whō Christ was sent backe again to Pilate, who at the length condemned him to be beatē with rods, and to be crucified. Now therfore Christ was condemned, that he might redeeme vs from eternall condemnation. His beating with rods is set downe Mat. 27.26.

His crucifying is that wherby he was fastned on wood, or on a crosse, that he might take the curse of the law from vs vpō himselfe. As it is written, cursed is euery one who hangeth on a tree. Mat. 27.38. Mar. 15.27. Luke. 23.33. 2. Cor. 13.4. Heb. 13.12. Iohn. 19.18.

Hitherto concerning the passion of Christ: now concerning his death, and those things which followed his death, namely his burying, and descending into hell.

The death of Christ is part of his obedience, when commending his soule to his father hee gaue vp the ghost on the crosse, to ratifie his Testament, and to loose the feare of death. Heb. 9.15.16.17. and 2.14.15.

The burying of Christ, is that whereby his body was layed into the new tombe. Mat. 27.59.60. Mar. 15.46. Actes. 13.29. 1. Cor. 15 4.

Christ was buried for foure causes.
- 1. That it might appeare that he was dead indeed.
- 2. That hee might bury our sinnes with himselfe.
- 3. That we might with him be buried to sinne. Rom. 6.4.
- 4. That he might sanctifie our sepulchres.

The descending of Christ to hell, is the very last degree of Christes humiliation, when he was kept downe in the graue vnder the bondes of death three dayes, and three nightes, as though he had bene vtterly ouercome. Actes. 2.24.27.29.30. Psal. 16.10. Ephes. 4.9. Mat. 12.40.

The end of this, is that he might abolish the sting of hell. 1. Cor. 15.55.

Hitherto concerning Christes humiliation: now concerning his exaltation.

Christes exaltation, is his state in which he was caried vp into the highest and vnspeakeable glory. Luke. 24.26. Phil. 2.9.

That doth comprehend both his resurrection, and manifestation of himselfe, fourtie dayes vpon the earth, and also his ascension into heauen, and his sitting at the right hand of God his father.

Christes resurrection, is that whereby he hauing ouercome death, and the dominion thereof, by his owne diuine power, he rose againe the third day from the dead, and liueth with God for euermore. 2. Cor. 13.4.1. Pet. 3.18. Rom 6.8.10. and 14.9.

There are foure endes and vses of the resurrection of Christ.

1. That he by his resurrection hath ouercome death, to the intent that he might make vs partakers of his righteousnesse, which by his death he hath purchased for vs. Rom. 4.25. 1. Pet. 1.1. Thess. 1.10.3.4.5.21. 1. Cor. 15.16.17.54.55. Or that he by his resurrection, hath fully confirmed to vs, the redemption & righteousnesse purchased for vs by his death.

2. That the deuill and death being ouercome, he might rule ouer the dead and the liuing Rom. 14.9.

3. That he by the power thereof might stirre vs vp to a new life. Rom. 6.4. Coloss. 3. 1. Ephes. 2.5.

4. That the resurrection of our head, is a pledge to vs of our glorious resurrection. 1. Cor. 15.12.13.14. Rom. 8.11.

The conuersation of Christ vpō the earth fourtie dayes after his resurrection, was done to that end, that he might most certainly confirme his resurrection: so that no man might doubt of it. Actes. 1.3.

The ascension of Christ into heauen, is that whereby in body, he was visibly lifted from the earth, and was receiued vp into heauen. Mar. 16.19. Actes. 1.9. Iohn. 14.2.

The heauen into which Christ ascended, and into which he will take vs, Christ himself teaching vs it, Ioh. 14.2. is the house of his heauenly father, in which there are many dwelling places, the throne of God, the place of ioye: and it is not euery where, but in the highest heauēs, it is a place as. 2. Chron. 6.21.

And therefore we beleeue that Christs body, is not now on earth, much lesse euery where, but in heauen: Actes. 13.21. yet Christ shalbe with vs euen to the end of the world, by his Godhead, grace and spirit. Mat. 28.20.

There are three endes of Christes ascension.

- 1. Because he doth make intercession for vs before his father in heauen Heb. 9.24. and 10. 19. 1. Iohn. 2.1. Rom. 8.34.
- 2. Because we haue our flesh in heauen that we by that, as by a certaine pledge might be confirmed, that it shall come to passe, that he which is our head may lift vs his members to himselfe. Iohn. 14.2. and 20.17. Ephes. 2.6. or else, that he might prepare a place for vs, that where he is, we might be also.
- 3. Because he doth fill the Church with his spirite, and vnspeakeable power, and beautifie it, with diuers giftes. Iohn. 14.16. and 16.7. Ephes. 4.10.11. Psal. 68.19. or else, because he sendeth vs the holy spirite in steed of a mutuall pledge.

Hitherto concerning Christes ascension: now concerning his sitting at the right hand of God the father.

The sitting of Christ at the right hand of God his father, is the highest degree of Christ his glory, whilest he doth possesse all power, ouer all creatures, in heauen & earth, that the father might both worke and gouerne all things immediatly by him. Psal. 110. Actes. 2.30. and 3.21. and 7.56. 1. Cor. 15.27. Ephes. 1.20. Phil. 2.9. Heb. 1.34. Mat. 28.18.

That is attributed to the person, that is to say: not to one nature of Christ seuerally, but euen to whole Christ God and man.

For when the kingly office of Christ is noted by it, it ought to be taken of the whole person, or of both natures.

And Christ sitteth at the right hand of God his father, not euery where, but in heauen, as the Scripture plainly testifieth. Heb. 8.1.4. Eph. 1.20 Col. 3.1. Acts. 3.21. Heb. 1.3.

And that not till after his ascension. Mar. 16.19. 1. Pet. 3.22.

And the ascension of Christ into heauen, is one thing, his sitting at the right hand of God his father, is another thing. 1. Because his sitting is the end of his ascension: for therefore Christ ascended to heauen, that he might sit at the right hand of his father.

2. Because Christ doth perpetually sit at the right hand of his father: but he ascended but once in heauen.

3. Because we shall also ascend into heauen, but we shall not sit at the right hand of God.

Hitherto concerning the person of Christ: now concerning his office.

The office of Christ, is to bestow on the elect all things which are required to eternall saluation.

This office doth ioyntly belong to both natures in the person of Christ. Iohn. 6.3.53. Heb. 9.14. Actes. 20.28.

And as that dutie belongeth to both natures: so also the effectes, that is to say, the workes of the office are attributed to Christ accorrding to both natures. Heb. 3.2.3.4.5.6. and 9.14. Actes. 20.28.

But in the performing of euery effect or worke, some things doe pertaine to the diuine nature, other some to the humane nature. 1. Pet. 1.18. and 2.24. and 3.18.

For although euery effect or worke of the mediatour be one, because the person of the mediatour is but one: yet to the effecting of this worke there doe concurre two operations, that is to say, two actions, one of the Godhead, another of the manhood: the Godhead doing those things which belong to the Godhead, & the māhood doing those things, which belong to manhood; as the worke of a man is but one, but in performing it, there doth concurre, the action both of the soule and body, the soule doing those things which belōg to the soule, and the body doing those things, which belong to the body.

And as the natures, and properties of the same remaine distinct: so also the actions, and operations of the natures, so that either of them doth seuerally worke that which is proper to it, namely the word working that which belongeth to the word: & the flesh accōplishing that which belōgeth to the flesh.

The offices of Christ are three: his Prophecie, Priesthood, and Kingdome. Psal. 110. Heb. 7.2.3. and 13.20.

The Prophecie of Christ, is perfectly to deliuer the whole word of God to men. Heb. 1.1. Iohn. 1.16.17.18. Esay. 61.1.

Therefore he is called, the chiefe Prophet, teacher, & Apostle of our confession. Heb. 3.1.

Of his Prophecie there are two partes: namely the foreshewing of things to come, and doctrine.

Of doctrine there are two parts: the laying open of the Gospell, and the true interpretation of the law.

The laying open of the Gospell, is the first part of Christes doctrine, when he did lay open, the secret counsell, and all his fathers will concerning our redemption. Iohn. 1.18. and 15.15. Mat. 11.17.

The true interpretation of the law, is the other part of Christes doctrine, when he expounded the true meaning of Gods law. Mat. 5.20. and so forward.

Thus farre concerning the Propheticall office of Christ: now concerning his Priesthood.

The Priesthood of Christ, is to performe the workes of a Priest. Heb. 5.10.

Of Christs Priesthood there are two parts: the expiation of sinne, & intercession to God.

The expiation of sinne, is the first part of Christes Priesthood, when Christ offering to God his father, the onely sacrifice of his body, did pay the punishment for the sinnes of the elect, to redeeme them from all the power of the deuill. 1. Pet. 2.24. and 3.18. Esay. 53.12. 1. Iohn. 2.2. Rom. 3.25. Heb. 10.12. Whereupon also it is called redemption. As also the satisfying for sinnes.

And that is done two wayes: by merite, and by a powerfull working.

The merite of Christ is a full satisfaction for our sinnes, sufficiēt for all the men of the world, if all did receiue the same by faith.

The powerfull working of Christ, is that by which he doth certainly bestow on the beleeuers, benefites purchased by his merite for them, as for example, the forgiuenesse of sinnes, regeneration, the holy spirit, and eternall life, and doth preserue the same benefites in them, and endue them with perseuerance that they fall not from grace.

<u>Thus much concerning the expiation of sinne: now concerning intercession to God.</u>

Intercession to God, is the other part of Christes Priesthood, whilest that he causeth by the perpetuall memory of his sacrifice, that his father should receiue vs into grace.

<u>Hitherto concerning Christes Priesthood: now concerning the kingly office of Christ.</u>

The kingly office of Christ, is this, that he as the head gouerneth the Church. Psal. 2.6. Luke. 1.33. Mat. 28.18. Iohn. 10.28.

And he exerciseth that two wayes: one way, if we consider the Church by it selfe; another way, if we cōsider the enemies of the Church.

If we consider the Church by it selfe, he exerciseth his kingdome two wayes.

- 1. Because by his holy spirit he powreth heauenly giftes vpon vs, which are his members. Ephes. 4.10.11.12.
- 2. Because he gouerneth vs by his word and spirite.

If we consider the enemies of the Church of Christ, he exerciseth his kingly office also two wayes.

- 1. That he by his power doth defend, preserue, and mightily deliuer both vs and that saluation which he hath purchased for vs, against our enemies. Psal. 2.9 and 110.1.2. Iohn. 10.28.29.30. Ephes. 4.8.

- 2. Because he doth beat downe their enemies, vntill at the length he may fully & perfectly deliuer vs from them.

The vanquishing of the enemies is two wayes.
- 1. Because he doth depriue our enemies of all power, although they be neuer so strong and proud, as the deuill, and all the wicked.
- 2. Because he doth vtterly abolish other, as death. 1. Cor. 15.26.

Thus farre concerning the reuelation of doctrine: now concerning the foretelling of things to come.

The foretelling of things to come is a laying open of Gods will, by which God would foretell those things which shall be hereafter, as farre as it might be for our good to know them.

And that is either confirmed by an oth, or else it is without an oth.

The oth of God, is a confirming of the foreshewing of things to come, not because that foreshewing is doubtfull, but because God would so prouide for our infirmity, iudging of God according to the maner of men, that if any bee not contented with the bare wordes of God, the othes might suffice him.

Taulerus saith thus: O blessed are they, for whose sake God sweareth: ô miserable are they, who beleeue not God, whē he sweareth.

The bare foretelling, is that which hath no oth adioyned to it, but yet it is as certain as if God that had sworne, had done it. And therfore Philo sayd elegātly, all the words of God are othes, in respect of their certaintie, neither do they need any cōfirmatiō, as whose truth proueth and defendeth it by the effectes, as the shining of the natiue light being sēt forth.

Againe the foretelling of things to come, is either absolute, or with a condition.

The absolute foretelling is that which is without all condition, and that is prophecie or foretelling.

A prophecie or foretelling, is a reuealing of misteries or secret things which shall come to passe in their due time. Such were many foretellings of the Prophetes: of Christ concerning his owne passion, death & resurrection, concerning the ouerthrow of Ierusalem, cōcerning the end of the world, & cōcerning false Prophets: of Agabus, concerning the pestilēce to come, & of Paul concerning the restoring of the Iewes, and concerning Antichrist. &c.

Hitherto concerning the absolute foretelling of things to come.

The foretelling of things to come with condition, is that to which some certaine condition is annexed, which if it be present, the things foretold are done.

And that is either promise or threatning.

Gods promise is a foreshewing of good things to come, which God will giue vs if we also performe those things which he requireth of vs, or if we satisfie the condition, which he layeth vpon vs.

The promise of God is either spirituall, or bodily.

The spirituall promise, is that whereby God doth shew, that he will giue vs spirituall good things.

The bodily promise, is that whereby God doth shew, that he will giue vs bodily good things, as farre as it may be expedient for our saluation.

Againe the promise is either of the law, or of the Gospell.

The promise of the law, is a promise, which the law propoundeth, hauing a condition of perfect obedience annexed vnto it.

For the law precisely commandeth the condition to be fulfilled, neither otherwise performeth it the promises, then as the condition shalbe throughly performed.

Therfore the perfect fulfilling of the condition commanded by the law, should haue had a respect of merit, and should haue bene a cause of obtaining those rewards, which the law promiseth.

But the perfect fulfilling of the condition of the law cannot be performed by men corrupted with sinne.

The promise of the law, although it hath a condition adioyned vnpossible to be performed by a corrupted nature: notwithstanding it is not vnprofitable, or idle: for the vnpossible condition is therefore adioyned, that men might be admonished of their weakenesse, and they throughly vnderstanding the same might flye to Christ, by whō they being receiued into grace, and already hauing obtained iustification, might obtaine those same promises.

The promise of the Gospell, is a promise which the Gospell propoundeth, hauing the condition of faith adioyned to it.

For the Gospell promiseth forgiuenesse of sinnes, and eternall life, yet to the beleeuers onely.

The promise of the Gospell is vniuersall but to the beleeuers: for all which beleeue in Christ do receiue forgiuenesse of sinnes, and eternall life. Actes. 10.43. Iohn. 3.16.

But it doth not pertaine to the vnbeleeuers.

Thus much concerning the promise: now concerning the threatning.

Threatning, is a denouncing of euils to come, by which God will either chasten his, or punish the wicked, except they repent.

Therefore the condition of repentance is adioyned.

Threatning also is either spirituall or bodily.

Spirituall threatning, is that whereby God doth denounce, that he will send spirituall euils vpon vs.

Bodily threatning, is that whereby God doth denounce, that he will send bodily euils vpon vs.

Hitherto concerning the supernaturall manifestation of Gods will: now concerning his calling of vs.

Our calling, is a worke of Gods speciall prouidence, whereby God doth call men to some certaine end. Matth. 22.9. 1. Cor. 1.9. 1. Tim. 2.4.29.

And that calling is either to Christ, or to some office.

The calling to Christ, is that calling, wherby God doth inuite vs to Christ, that by him we might obtaine eternall life.

And that calling is two fold, either inward or outward.

The outward calling, is a calling which is done by the Ministers of Gods word.

And that is two fold, effectuall, or vneffectuall. Mat. 22.2.

The effectuall calling belongeth to the elect, in whose harts the word preached doth abide.

The vneffectuall calling, belongeth to the reprobate, in whose harts the word of God either findeth no abode, or else vanisheth away, so that it is become to them the sauour of death, and a matter of more grieuous condemnation.

Thus much concerning the outward calling: now concerning the inward.

The calling that is inward, is a calling, which is wrought by the holy spirit, by whō the father draweth vs, and giueth vs to his sonne. Iohn. 6.37.44. and 17.11.

Hitherto concerning our calling to Christ: now concerning our calling to some office.

The calling to some office, is the separating of a fit person to some office. Rom. 1.1.

Thus farre concerning our calling: now concerning Gods couenant.

Gods couenant is a bargaine which God hath made with me•, in which God promiseth to men some good, & requireth of them again, that they performe those things which he commandeth.

And that couenant is either eternall or temporall.

The eternall couenant is a couenant in which God promiseth men eternall life.

And that is two fold, the couenant of workes, or the couenant of grace.

The couenant of workes, is a bargaine of God made with men cōcerning eternall life, to which is both a condition of perfect obedience adioyned, to be performed by man, & also a threatning of eternall death if he shal not performe perfect obedience. Gene. 2.17.

The repetition of the couenant of workes is made by God, Exod. 19.5. Deut. 5.2. 1. King. 8.21. Heb. 8.9. and that chiefly for foure causes.

- 1. That God by all meanes might stirre vp men to performe obedience.
- 2. That euery mouth might be stopped, and all the world might be made subiect to the condemnation of God for not performing perfect obedience. Rom. 3.19.
- 3. That he might manifest mans sinne, and naughtinesse. Rom. 3.19.20. and 7.7.8.9.10.11.
- 4. That he might thrust vs forward to seeke to be restored in the couenant of grace. Gal. 3.22. and 5.23.

Thus much concerning the couenant of workes: now concerning the couenant of grace.

The couenant of grace is the reconciling of the elect with God, by the death of the only mediatour. Rom. 8.30. 2. Cor. 5.17.18.19.20.21. Heb. 9.15.

That onely mediatour is our Lord Iesus Christ, who onely doth reconcile vs to his father, by his satisfaction and merit. Gene. 3.15. and 11.35. Gal. 3.12.13.14. Gene. 15.18. & 17.2.10.11. Exod. 6.4. the Epistle to the Heb. Chap. 7.8.9. & 10. The couenant made with Abraham, is the couenant of grace. Actes. 3.25.

The couenant of grace is also called the Testament, because this reconciliation, was made and ratified by the death of the testatour Christ comming betweene. Heb. 9.16.17. Christ purchased reconciliation between his heauenly father and vs, by his death, and there withall left it vnto vs no otherwise thē parents dying doe leaue their goods to their children.

And that perpetually is one and the selfe same, if we consider the substance thereof: as there is but one Church in all ages, one true faith &

Religiō of Saints, one God, one mediatour Christ, but one sacrifice for sins, but one righteousnesse & redēptiō of the world, one manner for all the ages of the world to obtaine saluation, namely by faith in Christ. Heb. 13.8. Reuel. 13.8. 1. Tim. 2.5. Rom. 12. and 4.3. Ephes. 1.10. Rom. 9.5. Col. 1.18. Ephe. 2.21. Actes. 4.2. Mat. 11.27. Iohn. 14.6. Luke. 10.24. Iohn. 8 56. Gene. 3.15. and 22.18.

But by the circumstances, it is called the old or new Testament.

It is called the old Testament or couenant, because it was hid from the faithfull by diuers shadowes and figures before Christ was manifested in the flesh. Gene. 12.7. Heb. 9.4.18. Exod. 24.8.

It is called the new Testamēt or couenāt, because it is clearly manifested to the faithfull, by Christ himselfe shewed in the flesh. Heb. 8 6.

Therefore the faithfull in the old Testament, had Christ as yet couered in a type, or rather they looked for a true manifestation of him: but we haue him manifested indeede.

They had figures, we haue the thing it selfe: they did reioyce in outward and ceremoniall things, we triumph in spirituall, and the things signified, without types. Ierem. 31.31. Matth. 26.28. 1. Cor. 11.25. Heb. 8.9.10. and Chap. 9. and 10.

Of the couenant of grace there be two parts: the promise of grace, & the answering againe of a good conscience. The former respecteth God, the later respecteth the faithfull. Heb. 8.10.11.12.

The promise of grace is the first part of the couenant of grace, by which God promiseth freely his benefites purchased by Christ, vnto all those who beleeue in Christ.

The benefites purchased by Christ for vs, and promised in the Gospell, are these the giuing of the holy spirit, the communion with Christ, and our preseruation in this communion, and the giuing of eternall life.

The giuing of the holy spirite, is a benefite of God; by which he giueth vs his holy spirite, who maketh vs partakers of Christ, and of all his benefites.

Of the knowledge of the holy spirit, there be two parts, the first concerning the person of the holy spirite; the second, concerning his office.

If we consider his person, he is true God, equall with the father, and the sonne. Actes. 5.3.4. Gene. 1.2. Math. 28.19. Mar 16 15.

But the office of the holy spirite, is this, that by him the father, and the sonne, doe shew foorth their power, and execute the decrees of their will, in creating, sustaining, and mouing all things but chiefly in mouing the harts of those that heare Gods word, and in sanctifying and quickning the elect with eternall saluation.

Thus farre concerning the giuing of the holy spirite: now concerning our communion with Christ.

Our communion with Christ, is the benefit of God, whilest he giueth to the beleeuers Christ himselfe, and his merits that he might powerfully worke in them eternall life. Iohn. 3.16. Rom. 8.32.

That is also called, our ioyning, vnion, knitting together with Christ, our ingrafting into Christ, the eating of Christes flesh, the drinking of Christes bloud, the bringing of vs vnder one head, ioyning into one body, vnder one head, to wit, Christ, Ephes. 1.10. our washing in the bloud of Christ, the quickning of vs, the raysing of vs from the dead, the placing of vs in heauen together with Christ. Ephes. 2.5.6.

Now the communion of all Saintes with Christ, is one and the selfe same, that is to say, onely spirituall. There is not a bodily entrance, and remayning of Christ within the bodies of the Saints: neither doth Christ dwell spiritually in some, and bodily in other some: but in all beleeuers spiritually onely. And that is done by the holy spirit, who notwithstanding doth truly ioyne and knit together, by faith, all the godly and faithfull with the flesh of Christ, although it be lifted vp and remaine in heauen. 1. Cor. 12.13. By one spirit are all we baptized into one body, and all we drinke one drinke into one spirit. For one and the selfe same spirit, worketh that in all Baptismes, in all the holy Suppers, that we might be one with Christ, and ioyned spiritually to him. Ephes. 3.12. He dwelleth in our harts by faith. Ephes. 4. One body & one spirit. 1. Iohn. 4. By this we know that he dwelleth in vs, and we in him, because he giueth vs of his spirit. Rom. 8. If the spirit of him, which raised Iesus frō the dead dwell in you, he that raysed vp Iesus from the dead, shal also quicken your mortall bodies, by his spirite that dwelleth in you.

Irenaeus booke 3. Chap. 19. As one lumpe and one loafe, cannot be made of dry wheat, without moysture: so neither can we being many be made one in Christ without the water which is from heauen.

And it belongeth to all the elect and beleeuers onely, euen from the beginning to the end of the world. 1. Iohn. 3.24. and 1. Iohn. 4.13. Iohn. 14.23. and 15.1.2.3.4.5.6.

The parts of our communion with Christ are these, Iustification, and Regeneration, Adoption, and the freedome of the sonnes of God.

Iustification is a benefit of God, by which we being receiued by him into fauour are accounted iust. Rom. 5.19. Ephes. 2.8.9. Rom. 3. and 4. and 5.

The partes thereof are two: forgiuenesse of sinnes, and imputation of Christes righteousnesse.

The forgiuenesse of sinnes, is a benefit of God, whereby he pardoneth vs both the offence, and eternall punishments due vnto it for sinne. 2. Cor. 5.19.21. Iere. 31.34. Psal. 103.3.10.12. Rom. 7.24. and 8.1.2.3.

Of the forgiuenesse of sinnes there be two parts: the forgiuenesse of the offence, and the forgiuenesse of eternall punishment.

Therfore by one forgiuenes, both are remitted to wit, the offence, & the eternall punishment. For the iustice of God requireth that, because Christ hath satisfied for both to wit, for the offence, & the punishment. Therfore God should be vniust if he should onely forgiue vs the offēce, & not the punishmēt also. Therefore the Papistes erre, who say, that the offence only is remitted, and not the punishment, for which they will haue men to satisfie, when as they can by no meanes do it, but Christ hath fully satisfied for it.

The imputing of Christs righteousnesse, is a benefit of God, wherby God vouchsafeth to account Christs obediēce, by which he sustained for vs the punishments of sin, to be ours, euen as though we our selues had sustained those punishmēts for sins. Esa. 53.3 4.5. Rom. 4.3.5. Rom. 5.11.18. Col. 1.22. 2. Cor. 5.19.21.

Thus farre concerning iustification: now concerning Regeneration.

Regeneration, is a benefite of God, by which our corrupted nature is renewed to the image of God by the holy spirite. 2. Pet. 1.4. Tit. 3.5. Gal. 4.6. 2. Cor. 3.7.

That same is also called sanctification, and the gift of grace. Rom. 5. Also of schoolemen it is called an infused grace.

Regeneration is either begun, or perfected: the former belongeth to this life, the later to the life to come.

In regeneration are to be considered both the partes, and also the perpetuall adioynts.

Regeneration is both of the soule, and also of the body. 1. Thess. 5.23.

Regeneratiō of the soule, is that wherby the powers of ye soule are renued. Tit. 3.5. Gal. 4.6.

Of the regeneration of the soule there are two parts: enlightening, and repentance.

As there are two parts of the soule, vnderstanding, and will: so also regeneration is wrought in those same two partes. The enlightening belongeth to the vnderstanding, and repentance belongeth to the will. So Paule sayth, that in regeneration the image of God is renewed to the acknowledgement of the creatour. Coloss. 3. and to true righteousnesse and holinesse, Ephe. 4.23.

Enlightening is the first part of the regeneration of the soule, whereby the naturall darknesse being driuē forth, our mind is enlightned with true knowledge how to obtaine eternall life. Psal. 16.11. Col. 3. Rom. 12 2.

That is also called the annoynting of the holy spirit.

Of enlightening there are two partes: spirituall wisedome, and prudence. Spirituall wisdome, is the wholesome knowledge of faith & the misteries of saluatiō, ioyned with confidence in Christ. Eph. 1.17.18.

Spirituall prudence, is a wholesome knowledge of things commanded or forbidden, by the law of God, with a desire of the former, and shunning of the latter ioyned to it.

Thus much concerning enlightening: now concerning repentance.

Repētāce, is the other part of the regeneratiō of the soule, whereby our will is renewed, that it no longer willeth euill, but that which is good only. Rom. 6.4.5.6. Ephe. 4.22.23.24. 2. Cor. 5.7. Phil. 2.13. It is also called repentance and turning to God, by putting the part for the whole, it hath the former name truly of the first part: and the other of the latter part.

And that doth not proceede from our owne free will, which being lost by sin, there is no more will to goodnesse after the fall, & especially to eternall saluation, Gen. 6.5. But it is the gift of God.

There are two partes thereof, the mortification of the old man, and the quickning of the new man.

The mortification of the old man, is the first part of repentance, whereby sinne (so far as it may be in this life) is abolished in vs. Rom. 6.4.5.6. Coloss. 3.5.6.7.8.9.10. Rom. 8.13. It is called also the denying of our selues. Also the putting off of the old man. Coloss. 3.9.10.

The partes thereof, are both the acknowledgement and confession of sinne, and also the detestation, and hatred of sinne: next a profitable sadnesse for sinne.

The ackhowledgement of sinne, is when we acknowledge that we haue sinned. Ierem. 3.2.13.

The confession of sinne, is that whereby we openly testifie that we haue sinned, & offended God. 1. King. 8.47. 2. Sam. 24.10. And that is either publicke or priuate.

The priuate confession, is that which is done priuatly of euery one, euen within his own priuate house. And that is either to God onely, or to man. To man either to the Minister of the word, or to some faithfull friend.

Publicke confession, is that which is done publickely with the whole Church.

Publicke confession, is either of the whole Church, or of one, or many in the face of the Church.

The detestation of sinne, is when we accuse & condemne both the sinnes committed by vs, and our selues also for our sinnes sake. 1. Cor. 11.31. If we would iudge our selues, we should not be iudged by the Lord.

The hatred of sinne is a perpetuall shunning of sinne. For to hate sinne, is to turne away from it, and to shunne it. Nehem. 9.35. Ierem. 36.3. Ezech. 14.6.

A profitable sadnesse, is true feare, and grief of conscience for sinnes committed, by which we offend God, ioyned with the true hatred of sinne. Esay. 66.2. 2. Cor. 7.11. Ioel. 2.12.13. Deut. 4.29. Ionas. 3.8. 2. King. 22.19.

Hitherto concerning the mortification of the old man: now concerning the quickening of the new man.

The quickning of the new mā, is the other part of repentance, whereby a new spirituall life is raysed vp in vs. Gal. 2.19. Rom. 6.10.11.

And that same is called our resurrection with Christ.

Of this there be two parts: the comfort of the conscience, and spirituall gouernement.

The comfort of the conscience, is the true ioy of a contrite cōscience in God, hauing receiued forgiuenesse of sins by faith, through Christ. Psal 51.10.14. Rom. 5.1. Esay. 57.15.16.17.18. and 61.1. Esay. 49 13.

The spirituall gouernement, is the other part of quickning by which God leadeth by his spirit the regenerate, in the right way of his commandements, so that they liue no longer to sin, but to God• and do lead a new life. Rom. 6 throughout. Also 7. and 8. where he speaketh largely of sanctification, or regeneration. Dauid very often prayeth to God for this spirituall gouernement, chiefly Psal. 119.33.34.35. and euery where throughout the whole Psalme. So Psal. 25.8.9.10.

Thus far concerning the regeneratiō of the soule: now concerning the regeneration of the body.

The regeneration of the body, is that by which the body is made obediēt to the spirit, being regenerated. Rom. 12.1.

Therfore there is both a mortification, and quickning of the body also. Rom. 6.12. &c.

The parts of the regeneration of the body are two: the bridling of the affections, and the ruling of the moueable members,

The bridling of the affections is the first part of the regeneratiō of the body, by which the affectiōs of the body are tamed, that they might obey reason regenerated.

The ruling of the moueable mēbers, is the other part of the regeneration of the body, by which all the members of the body are ruled, lest being thrust forward by the rēnāts of corrupted lusts, they shuld do any thing cōtrary to the cōsent of the mind & will regenerated.

The testimony of regeneration, is a holy, and iust life.

O how many are there, who by their wicked life do openly shew, that they are not regenerated!

An vpright man, & a corrupted mā, a regenerated man, & an vnregenerated man differ by a rationall respect, and not in subiect and truth of being.

Hitherto concerning the parts of regeneration: the perpetuall adioynts thereof remaine.

The spirituall warfare, or battell, and victory of the Saints, are things continually accompanying regeneration.

The spiritual battel or warfare, is ye battel of a regenerated mā, by which he fighteth against the deceipts of the deuill, the bad exāples of the world, the sollicitings of his owne flesh, as the causes of sinne, & resisteth them stoutly. Rom. 7.8▪ and so forward. Gal. 5.16.17.

The victory of the saints, is a victory, wherby the Saints doe through Christ ouercome the snares of the deuill, of the world, and their owne flesh.

Hitherto concerning regeneration: now concerning adoption and the freedome of the sonnes of God.

Adoption, is a benefit of God, by which he receiueth vs for Christes sake, to be his sonnes, and maketh vs heires, of heauen, and eternall life with him. Rom. 8.15.16.17. Gal. 3.26. Ephes. 1.5. Iohn. 1.12.

Adoption is two fold: imperfect is that which we haue in this life: of this it is spoken to the Romanes; For ye haue not receiued the spirit of bondage againe to feare, but the spirite of the adoption of sonnes, by which we crye Abba father. And they already haue obtained this adoption, who haue receiued Christ by faith. Iohn. 1.12. The other adoption is perfect, which in the resurrection shalbe giuen: of that it is spoken in the same Chapter to the Romanes; Euery creature sigheth, and waiteth for the reuealing of the sonnes of God. Moreouer euen we also hauing the first fruites of the spirite, doe sigh within our selues, wayting for the adoption, and redemption of our bodies.

Thus farre concerning adoption: now concerning the freedome of the sonnes of God.

The freedome of the sonnes of God, is the deliuering of vs by Christ, from a spirituall bondage. Gal. 5.1.

The freedome of the sonnes of God, is either inward, or outward.

The inward freedome· is that which belongeth to the inward life. Iohn. 8.31.36.

And that is two fold: freedome from eternall bondage, and freedome from the bondage of sinne.

Freedome from eternall bondage, is that by which we are freed from the power and tiranny of the deuill, and from condemnation, and eternall death. Iohn. 8.36.

By this we are comforted in the conflict of conscience with the iudgement of God.

Freedome from the bondage of sin, is that by which we are deliuered from the dominiō of sinne, that sin may no longer raigne ouer vs, but that we being iustified, and endued with the holy spirit, might liue to righteousnesse and vnto God. Iohn. 8.34. 2. Cor. 3. where the spirit of the Lord is, there is liberty. Rom. 6.6. and so forward euen to the end. 2. Pet. 2.19. Galat. 5.13.

Thus much concerning inward freedome: now concerning outward freedome.

The outward freedome, is that which pertaineth to the outward life. And it is called Christian liberty, because it belongeth to Christians onely.

And that is two fold, freedome from the lawes of Moses, and freedome in indifferent things.

Freedome from the lawes of Moses, is that by which Christians are loosed from the ceremoniall, & Iudiciall lawes of Moses, namely, so farre forth as they onely pertaine to the ciuill gouernement vnder Moses. 1. Cor. 9.1.19. 2. Cor. 3.17. Heb. 9.10.

For such lawes which belong to the law of nature, and by which all nations are bound, are not abrogated.

Freedome in indifferent things, is that by which Christians are free, in the vse of indifferent, and meane things. 1. Cor. 9.1.

Things indifferent or meane things, are those, which are neither commanded, nor forbidden by God but are deliuered, and instituted by men.

Such are the ceremonies instituted by humane authority, for good orders sake.

These may be kept or omitted, by the power of Christian liberty.

They may indeed be obserued in this respect; namely, for the preseruing of concord, and auoyding of the offence of the weake. Rom 14.15.16. 1. Cor. 8.1.9. & 11.29. 2. Cor. 11.12. but so that always there be no false opinion, namely, 1. of merit, as though the obseruing of them, might merit forgiuenesse of sinnes.

2. Of worship, as though God would be worshipped with thē, cōtrary to his expresse word; Mat. 15. In vayne they worship me▪ according to the commandements of men. Also. Ezech; 20. Walke in my commandements, and not in the precepts of your fathers.

3. Of perfection as though the obseruing of them could make vs perfect.

4. Of necessity, as though it were necessary that they should be obserued for conscience sake, & as though the conscience were hurt, vnlesse they were obserued, when as yet notwithstanding no lawes binde the consciences of men, except the lawes of God onely.

They also may be omitted without sinne, where no danger of offence is, & without the shew of denying the truth, and without the omitting of a necessary confession.

But they do sinne, whosoeuer neglecting these things, do breake such ceremonies, in reformed Churches.

Therefore indifferent things, according to the circumstances are either lawfull or vnlawfull Rom. 14.20.21. 1. Cor. 8.13.

But here now where there is contention & contrariety of circumstances, those which are lesse, must giue place to those which are of greater importance, the lesse number must giue place to the more. Rom. 14.21.

Notwithstanding we must take heed, lest those things be iudged indifferent which are not indifferent.

Such are those which are both superstitious, and wicked things.

Superstitious things, are those, the obserning whereof, is ioyned with a false opinion of merit, worship, perfection and necessity.

Wicked things, are those which are flatly contrary to Gods commandements, of which sort are many traditions of the Pope, as the abuse of the Lordes Supper, prayer to the dead, the worshipping of images, the law of single life, holy dayes dedicated to Saintes, images made for Religions sake, that is to say, that they may serue to the vse of Religion, or that they might be worshipped, or that holy things might be represented by them. For God will not haue images serue to this end: but he will haue all men to be taught by his word. And the monuments, by which heauenly things are represented, are the Sacraments onely, not painted, or grauen, but administred. For Christ doth not say, paint this, but do this, that is to say, breake the bread, & so forth, in remembrance of me.

The vse of the doctrine cōcerning Christiā liberty is two fold.
- 1. That we might learne in what things our righteousnesse doth properly consist.
- 2. That we might know what to iudge of ceremonies, namely that righteousnesse is not to be sought for in them, but that we freely by Christ obtaine righteousnesse, and forgiuenesse of sinnes, not for the obseruation of any ceremonies, or traditions of men.

<u>Hitherto concerning our communion with Christ: now concerning our preseruation in this communion.</u>

The preseruation of the elect in their communion with Christ, is a benefite of God, whereby he doth preserue the elect euen to the end, that they should not perish, but that they should remaine in the fellowship of Christ. 1. Pet. 1.5.

The parts thereof are, consolation, the hearing of the electes prayers, defence against their enemies, deliuerance out of dangers, and the gift of perseuerance.

Consolation, is a benefit of God, whereby he doth strengthen vs, to the suffering of aduersities, with an vnspeakeable ioye of hart ioyned thereunto. Psal. 94.19. and 119.76.77. 2. Cor. 1.3. 1. Cor. 10.13.

And that is either common in euery affliction, or particular in death.

The common consolation in euery affliction, is manifold.
- 1. Because affliction proceedeth from the diuine prouidence of our most mercifull and heauenly father. 2. Sam. 16.10. Ier. 14.22.
- 2. Because affliction serueth to the good & saluation of the elect. Rom. 8.28. Psal. 119.71. Reuel. 3.10.
- 3. Because affliction bringeth foorth patience Iam. 12.3. Rom. 5.3.
- 4. Because they who suffer affliction for godlinesse, and the truths sake are blessed. Matth. 5.10.11. Luke. 6.22. Iam, 1.12. 1. Pet. 3.14. and 4.14.
- 5. Because affliction, bideth but for a while. 2. Cor. 4.17.
- 6. Because God himselfe putteth an end to affliction. 1. Cor. 10.13.
- 7. Because affliction cannot separate vs frō Gods loue. Rom. 8.39.
- 8. Because affliction is not a testimony of Gods wrath.
- 9. Because affliction is a testimony of Gods loue. Prou. 3.11.13. Heb. 12.6. 1. Pet. 2.19.20.

- 10. Because he that is proued by affliction, shall receiue the crown of life, which God hath promised to those that loue him. Iam. 1.122. Tim. 2.11. Mat 5.12. Reuel. 2.10.
- 11. Because it cannot ouerthrow the elect. 2. Cor. 4.8.
- 12. Because the end of affliction wilbe ioyfull Luke. 6.21 Mat. 5. vers. 4.
- 13. Because other Saints also haue bene subiect alwayes to afflictio. Iam. 5.11. Mat. 5.12.
- 14. Because the spirite of God resteth on those that beare affliction. 1. Pet. 4.14.
- 15. Because by affliction we must enter into the kingdome of God. Rom. 14.22.
- 16. Because by affliction we must be conformable to the image of the sonne of God. Rom. 8.28. 1. Pet. 4.13.
- 17. Because they that beare afflictiō shall not be cōdemned with the world. 1. Cor. 11.32.
- 18. Because Christ himselfe hath sustained affliction. Heb. 12.2.
- 19. Because the eternall ioye which we shall reape in the kingdome of God, shall excell by many degrees the griefe of afflictiō in this life.
- 20. Because affliction shall not endure for euer.
- 21. Because by affliction our heauēly father hath appointed to make triall of his elect.
- 22. Because by daily affliction, we being admonished of our weaknesse and fraylty, might be hūbled, & so being humbled, we do learne to call for Gods assistance.
- 23. Because in affliction, we haue experience of the louing presence of God.
- 24. Because affliction is a token of obtayning eternall inheritance.
- 25. Because our hope is strēgthened by affliction.
- 26. Because by affliction we learne due obedience to God.
- 27. Because affliction doth get in vs contēpt and lothing of this present life.
- 28. Because affliction admonisheth vs of the vanity of this present life.
- 29. Because affliction doth inuite vs to the meditation of the life to come.
- 30. Because at the lēgth God freeth vs from all euill.

Hitherto concerning the common comfort in euery affliction: now concerning the particular comfort in death.

Comfort against death is likewise manifold.
- 1. Because we doe not liue or dye to our selues, but to God Rom. 14.8.
- 2. Because Christ is to vs both in life and in death an aduantage. 1. Phil. 12.
- 3. Because Christ is our resurrection, and life: & they who beleeue in him although they were dead, yet shall they liue. Ioh. 11.25.
- 4. Because God mitigateth and shortneth, to his seruants the sorrowes of death.
- 5. Because our death turned into sleepe, is a fulfilling of the mortification of our flesh: & he who is dead is free frō sin. Rom. 6.7.
- 6. Because we know, that if the tabernacle of this our earthly house we dissolued, we shall haue a building of God, namely a dwelling place not made with hands, but eternall in the heauens. 2. Cor. 5.1.
- 7. Because we dying godlily go to Christ, which is best of all for vs. Phil. 1.23.
- 8. Because this way of all flesh is sanctified by the death of Christ.
- 9. Because if at any other time in suffering the griefes of this life, yet especially in the agony of death, the power of comfort, which the spirite of Christ ministreth, doth beyōd all account ouercome the sorrowes of death.
- 10. Because the flesh indeede is weake, but the spirit is ready. Mat. 26.41. Therfore the whole man doth not feare death indeede, but his meaner part, namely the flesh.
- 11. Because the desire that we haue clearely to behold God, and to be deliuered from whole sinne, doth greatly diminish, & mitigate the feare and sorrow of death.
- 12. Because our loue towardes the faithfull, who ouercōming death haue gone before vs, and with whom we greatly desire to be ioyned in one country, ought to be no lesse, then it is towardes them whom we leaue aliue behind vs in this miserable exile, and from whom we are loth to be separated, who must yet notwithstanding by and by follow after vs.

- 13. Because we do so euidently, and so often perceiue the mercy of God towardes our children being dead, therefore it becommeth vs, to be of a resolute mind, especially sith we know that we are sealed with the pledge of the holy spirite.
- 14. Because we must not make greater account of this naturall life, then of the spirituall: for so it is meet that the desire hereof might lessen the feare of death.
- 15. Because we certainly know, that the soule indeede is immortall, and is caried by Angels to the assembly and congregation of the first borne, who are written in heauē. Luke. 16.22. Heb. 12.13. And we know that the body resteth in the earth: neither indeed hath one vnfitly called the graue the hauen of the body.
- 16. Because we beleeue the resurrection of the body and life eternall.
- 17. Because as in the whole life, so in the agony of death, God doth not suffer his seruants to be tēpted aboue that which they are able to beare, but doth giue, euen the issue with the tēptation. 1. Cor. 10.13. That in deed is a wonderfull thing, which Gregory saith in his Morals; Some dye laughing. But we had rather say, that death is ouer-come in vndergoing it manfully.
- 18. Because we must not thinke so carefully of a quiet death, as of an holy life. For as Augustine said excellently: We must not thinke that death euill, before which hath gone a holy life. And as the same man sayth; He cannot dye euilly, who hath liued well: and he hardly dyeth well, who hath liued euilly.
- 19. Because death neuer is altogether vntimely, whether we respect the good or wicked. For the godly are called before the time, that they should no lōger be vexed of the euill: but the euill and wicked are taken away, that they should no lōger persecute the good. As the same Augustin saith.
- 20. Because this life is filled with so many & great miseries, that death compared with it is taken to be a remedy, & not a punishment: as Ambrose iudged.
- 21. Because he that hath an extreme feare to dye, doth not hope to liue a•••r death: as saith Chrysostome.
- 22. Because it is better to offer that (I meane our spirit) for a free will offering to God, which otherwise we are bound to restore, because it is his due: as Chrysostome saith.
- 23. Because as death is euill to the euill, so it is good to the good, to whom all things worke together for good.
- 24. Because death is the way to life: as Ambrose wisely saith.

- 25. Because this death is the reparing of life: as the Church singeth.
- 26. Because as Bernard saith: The death of the iust is good, by reason of the rest it bringeth with it: better because it reneweth vs: best, because it putteth vs out of daunger. And as the same man saith, the death of sinners, is bad, worser, worst of all: but the death of the good, is good, better, best of all.
- 27. Because that death is good, which taketh not away life, but trāslateth it into a better estate. This a sentēce of the same Bernard.
- 28. Because as the same man also witnesseth, death hath freed vs from death, life from errour, grace from sinne.
- 29. Because faithfull men take death to be but a name onely: as saith Chrysostome.
- 30. Because God ruleth death, that it cannot be a cause of any euill.

<u>Hitherto concerning comfort: now concerning the rest of the benefites.</u>

The hearing of the elects prayers, is a benefite of God, whilest the elect praying in Christes name, God performeth vnto them all things which profit their saluation. Iohn. 9.31. Psal. 145.18.19. Iohn. 14.13.14. and 15.16.

Defence against enemies, is a benefite of God, whilest he so defendeth the elect against their spirituall and bodily enemies, that by no meane, they can hinder their saluation.

Deliuerance out of dangers, is a benefite of God, whilest he doth often beyond all hope of man, deliuer his elect being in distresse, that so (trying his presence in their perils) they might reioyce in him.

The gift of perseuerance, is a benefite of God, whilest he doth so seale in the elect the grace of Iesus Christ by the holy spirite, that they continue in it, euen to the end, and can not fall from it. Rom. 11.29. Matth. 24.24.1. Iohn. 2.19.27. 2. Pet. 2.18. Iohn. 10.28. Rom. 8.35. Luke. 22.32.

<u>Hitherto concerning our preseruation in this communion with Christ: now concerning the gift of eternall life.</u>

The gift of eternall life, is a benefite of God, purchased for vs by Christ, when after this life God will giue the elect, that they may liue with him for euer.

<u>Hitherto concerning the promise of grace: now concerning the answering againe of a good conscience.</u>

The answering again of a good consciēce is the other part of the couenant of grace, whereby the beleeuers do againe promise to God, that they will in true saith receiue his benefites, and that they will serue him in true righteousnesse and holynesse, the better to declare their thankefulnesse towardes him.

Hitherto concerning the eternall couenant: now concerning the temporall couenaut.

The temporall couenant is a couenant, in which God promiseth men temporall good things. Of this sort was the couenant which God made with mankind after the flood, that he would not destroy the world any more with a flood. Gene. 9.8. and so forward.

And that standeth vpon the eternall couenant, & is as it were belonging thereunto.

Hitherto concerning Gods couenant: now concerning the diuine signe.

The diuine signe, is that which of it selfe doth cause some diuine thing to come into mās mind, besides that shew which it offereth vnto the senses. Or else, it is some thing offering it selfe vnto the senses, which putteth men in minde of some other thing, which is ioyned with that signe.

A signe is either naturall or giuen.

A naturall signe is a signe which by nature hath that selfe same thing in it which it signifieth. Of this sort is the rainebow, signifying either showres or faire weather, if it be considered naturally.

A signe giuen, is a signe, which doth not by nature signifie that whereof it is a signe, but it signifieth by the appointment and will of God: as the rainebow is a signe by the appointment of God, that the world shall not perish with a flood.

The signe giuen, is either a miracle or a Sacrament.

A miracle is a signe effected beyond the order of nature. Exod. 3.2. and 14.21.22.23. Dan. 34.9. and 6.22. Mat. 14.19.20.

Therefore if any thing be done according to the order and course of nature, it is not miraculous, but naturall.

There are two endes of miracles: the one, that God by them might manifestly shew forth his power. Exodus 19. and 20. Dan. 3.

The other, that by them as by seales, he might confirme true doctrine. Mat. 16.17.

It is true indeed that in miracles the order of nature by the ouerruling power of God is interrupted, but neuer destroyed or ouerthrowen, throwen, neither are the essences of those things destroyed, although the forme be sometime chaunged. So when the Sunne stood while Ioshua fought, when it returned backe when Ezekiah was sicke, the order of nature was interrupted, not ouerthrowen: for afterward the Sunne kept the same course againe, which was giuen to it in the creation. Yet neuer thelesse the essence of the Sunne remained. When the sea was deuided, the course of the sea was interrupted: but the worke being firnshed which God had decreed, it returned againe to the former course, and continued the same: yea the very essence of the sea remained. When Aarons rod was made a Serpent, it was not the taking away of the substance, but a changing of it. So the water in Cana of Galile, the substance was not taken away, but it was turned into wine.

Now God worketh most freely in the effecting of miracles: for be himselfe hath most freely put that order into nature, therefore also whē he will he can most freely interrupt it. Furthermore because he is not bound to the order of nature, he may interrupt it as it pleaseth him.

And although God can doe all things, yet must not miracles be euery where alledged, especially where men cannot be well assured of Gods will, neither yet where no necessitie is: as for example, in the holie Supper men may not imagine miracles, as though the body of Christ were supernaturally and miraculously in the bread: because Christ hath no where said that he would haue it so. No where, I say, hath he sayd, that he would be in the bread. Furthermore it is not of necessity: for Christ may become ours, although he descēd not into the bread, or with the bread to be thrust into our mouthes.

Thus farre concerning a miracle: now concerning a Sacrament.

A Sacrament, is an outward signe, which God ioyneth to his couenant, which he hath made with men.

And that is either of an eternall, or temporall couenant.

A Sacrament of an eternall couenant, is a Sacrament, whereby God doth confirme the promise of eternall life.

And that is either of the couenāt of works, or of the couenant of grace.

The Sacrament of the couenant of works, is a Sacrament, which God gaue our first parents in the state of their first integrity.

And that was two fold, the tree of life, and the tree of the knowledge of good and euill.

The tree of life was a Sacrament of the couenant of workes, whereby that life was signified, which man should haue liued, if he had stood in the obedience of God. Gene. 2.9.

The tree of the knowledge of good and euill, was a Sacrament by which was signified to man, in how good estate he was whilest he performed obedience to God his creator: and into how euill and miserable estate he should cast himselfe if he obeyed not God. Gen. 2.17. & 3.7.8.9.10.11.

<u>Hitherto concerning the sacrament of the couenant of workes: now concerning the Sacrament of the couenant of grace.</u>

The Sacrament of the couenant of grace, is a seale of the righteousnesse of faith. Rom. 4.11.

Or else, the Sacrament of the couenant of grace is a Sacrament by which the faithfull are both admonished, and also are made sure that the couenant of grace, and all the benefites of God which are promised in this couenant, doe not onely belong to others, but seuerally to euery one of them, who doe vse the Sacrament according to Gods ordinance.

It is also called a Mysterie, because it signifieth secret thinges, and such as are vnknowne to them who haue not beene taught out of the worde of God concerning the signification and vse of them: because in a mysterie one thinge is seene, and an other is meant.

The Vbiquitaries doe thinke it therefore to be called a mystery, because the manner of the bodily receiuing of it is vnsearchable: but this is a false cause, because the bodily receiuing hath no foundation in the Scripture, but it is the deuise and imagination of men. Furthermore, this manner is manifested to vs, namely that it is spirituall, and that the receiuing is done by faith.

Both the Word and Sacraments doe lead our faith to Christ, as to the only foundation of our saluation.

Therefore in the Sacraments is propeunded, offered, giuen and sealed, no other thing then is promised and preached in the Gospell, but one and the selfe same thing, namely, Christ with his benefites. In the Sacraments we receiue no other thing, then in the simple worde, namely Christ with his benefites.

And the receiuing of Christ, whether it be in the simple worde, as in Iohn. 6. or in the Sacraments, is one and the selfe same, to wit, spirituall, that is to say, which is wrought in vs by the power of the holy spirite, and by the onely instrument of faith. The receiuing of Christ in the worde and Sacramentes doe not differ indeede: for in both there is the same thing and the same substance, to wit, Christ with his benefites. It doth not differ in the manner, for it is spirituall in them both. The difference is not in the instrument by which wee receiue it, for in them both faith is the instrument to receiue it by. What then is the difference betweene the receiuing of Christ in the simple worde, and in the Sacraments? The outwarde forme onely: to wit, because in the Sacraments bodily signes are ioyned with the word of promise. In the simple worde God dealeth with vs by preaching, and by our eares onely: but in the Sacramentes he vseth beside, such signes as offer themselues to the rest of the senses also: whereby it commeth to passe, that the communicating of Christ by the Sacraments, is more forcible and plaine, then by the simple word only.

There are two partes of the Sacrament of the couenaunt of grace: namely the earthly matter, and the outwarde action, or the outwarde rite. Genes. 17.11. Exod. 12.8. and so forwarde. Matth. 3.11. and 28.9. Matth. 26.26. and so forward. 1. Cor. 11.23.24.25.

The earthly matter alone, is not a perfect and whole Sacrament, but there must be adioyned to it the outwarde action or ceremonie, or the vse of the earthly matter appointed by Christ.

For nothing hath the force of a Sacrament, except there be adioyned to it the vse of it, according to Christes institution.

The earthly matter in the Sacrament, is a signe or token, by which vnder a certaine promised similitude, a heauenly matter is signified and represented to the faithfull, that so they might bee assured, that the heauenly matter is as certaine spiritually present, as they doe certainely see the earthly matter, to be bodily present before their eies. Gen. 17.11. Rom 4 11. Eze. 36 25.

Christ himselfe by the holy spirite, doth make the thinges promised present to our faith: and faith receiueth them.

Faith worketh not that presence: but Christ himselfe worketh it.

The heauenly matter signified in the Sacrament by the earthly matter, is the new Testament or couenant of grace, in the bloud of Christ.

Therefore we must not respect the minister and earthly elements, but turne the eyes of our fayth to the thinges promised.

Wherefore also the earthly matter by a manner of speaking, both vsuall in the Scripture and Church, and also plaine in it selfe, is also oft-times called by the name of the heauenly matter: because the heauenly matter is signified and meant by the earthly. Exod. 24.8. The bloud of the sacrifices is called the bloud of the couenant. Genes. 17.10. Circumcision is called the couenant. Exod. 12.11. The Paschall Lambe is called the Passeouer. Titus 3.5. Baptisme is called the washing of regeneration.

Now howe these speeches concerning the Sacramentes ought to be vnderstoode and expounded, the Scripture it selfe doeth declare, because the earthly matter is a signe of the couenant. Genes. 17.11. Because it is a seale of the righteousnesse of fayth. Rom. 4.11. Because it is a remembrance of Christes death.

And it is so called by a metaphor, in which the signe is eyther put for the thing signified, or is called by the name of the thing signified.

Hitherto concerning the earthly matter: now concerning the outwarde action in a Sacrament.

The outward action in a Sacrament, that is to say, a rite or ceremonie which we must obserue in yᵉ Sacramēt according to the institution Christ, is a signe of the inward action. Deut. 30.6. Matth. 3.11. Rom. 6.3. 1. Cor. 6.11. Col. 2.11. Act. 22.16.

This action is two fold: one of the minister administring the Sacrament, the other of a faythfull man vsing a Sacrament.

The action of the Minister administring the Sacrament is two folde: the sanctification of the earthly matter: and the administring of the same earthly matter?

The sanctifying of the earthly matter, is an action of the minister, in the which by Gods commaundement, hee appointeth the earthly matter to a holy vse.

Therefore the rehearsing of the wordes of the institution of the Sacrament is necessarie, both that the manner of instituting the Sacrament may bee layde open, as also that by it the earthly matter may bee sanctified and consecrated to a holy vse, because therein the commaundement of God is contayned. Therefore Augustine sayth; The worde commeth to the element, and so there is a Sacrament. 1. Corinth. 11.23.24.25.

The administring of the earthly matter, is the other action of the minister, whereby is meant, that God doth as certainely offer and giue the benefites that he hath promised, as we do certainely see that the earthly matter is offered and giuen vs by the minister of the word. 1. Cor. 11.23.

The minister of the worde distributeth and offereth the earthly matter: but Christ himselfe distributeth and offereth the heauenly matter. Matth. 3.11. I baptize you with water, there is an other who baptizeth with the holy spirite.

Hitherto concerning the action of the minister that administreth the Sacrament.

The action of a faithfull man vsing a Sacrament is also two folde: namely, the receiuing of the earthly matter, and thankesgiuing.

The receiuing of the earthly matter, is the action of a faithfull man vsing the Sacramēt, whereby he receiueth the earthly matter, to signifie that he doth so certainely receiue spiritually the benefits that God hath promised, as he doth certainly receiue bodily the earthly matter. Rom. 4.11. Matth. 26.26.

We receiue the worde of the promise of grace, and the earthly matter from the mouth and hand of the minister: but we receiue the heauenly matters from the hande of Christ himselfe.

The outward receiuing is wrought in the body: the inward is only wrought by faith & by the powerfull working of the holy spirit in our harts: for the inward receiuing comprehendeth iustification and regeneration.

We receiue the earthly matter by the body, that is to say, by the members, actions, & senses of the body, by the eies, eares, handes, mouth & stomacke, sight, hearing, touching, tast, and smell: but we receiue the heauenly matters by faith, and the powerfull working of the holy spirite in our hearts.

And therefore not onely the faithfull, but euen infidels receiue the earthly matter: but the faithfull onely receiue the heauenly matter.

Thankesgiuing is the action of a faithfull man vsing the Sacraments, whereby he with his mouth and heart giueth thanks to Christ, for the whole worke and benefite of his redemption. 1. Cor. 11.25.26.

These therefore are the partes of a Sacrament, which are required to the perfecting of euery Sacrament, by which the couenant of grace is sealed vp: with which if in the true vse thereof, the heauenly matters and the inwarde action be ioyned together, this coniunction is called a Sacramentall vnion, which is also the cause of the speeches proper to a Sacrament.

Therefore the Sacramentall vnion, is a spirituall ioyning together of the Sacrament, with those things whereof it is a Sacrament, or else it is a ioyning together of the signes and things, that is to say, of the earthly matter with the heauenly, and of the outwarde action with the inward action.

This vnion is not naturall and locall, but spirituall and belonging to couenants, and hauing respect to others, which is in the diuine disposing of the signe to the thing it selfe: and in the spirituall offering and receiuing of things truely ioyned with the bodily offering and receiuing of signes.

As therfore there are two parts of a Sacrament: so also of the sacramentall vnion.

The first part, is the vniting of the earthly matter with the heauenly.

It is not necessary, that this heauenly matter, be substantially and bodily in the earthly matter, or in that place in which the earthly matter is, because this vnion is meerly spirituall.

Neither doth it follow, if Christ be not bodily present on the earth in the earthly matter, or in the place in which the earthly matter is, that therefore he is not present, because that indeede is truly present which is present spiritually.

The other part of the sacramentall vnion, is the ioyning together of the outward action with the inward action.

For in the right vse of the Sacrament, the offering and receiuing of the signe and thing signified is ioyned together: the offering, & receiuing of the sign indeede is bodily, by the hand of the minister: but the offering and receiuing of the thing signified, is spirituall, through true faith by the hād of Christ himselfe.

For a Sacrament, is not onely an earthly, and bodily action, but a heauenly and spirituall action also, in which not only the earthly matter, which is on earth, but also those things which are in heauen, which are in God, and which are in the hearts of the faithfull, are present with vs.

And the holy spirit ioyning vs together with Christ, doth couple vs, euen we being most farre asunder, as in regard of distance of place, much more nearly and straightly, then either the soul is ioyned with the body, or the vine with the braunches.

Hitherto concerning the parts of the couenant of the Sacrament of Grace: the ends follow.

There are seuen ends of the Sacrament of the couenant of Grace.

1 That it might be a remembraunce of Gods benefits, both already offered, and hereafter to be offered, that is to say, that it might put the faithfull in minde of Christs benefites, eyther already bestowed, or hereafter to be bestowed on them. So the Passeouer was a remembrance not only of the deliueraunce out of Egypt already past, but also of the deliueraunce to come by Christ. So the holy Supper is a remembrance, not onely of our redemption made vpon the erosse: but also of that which is to be performed when he shall come to iudge the quick & the dead, and shall fully deliuer his elect from sin, and all their enemies. Luk. 21.28.

2 That our faith might thereby be increased, exercised and strengthened.

3 That by it we might be stirred vp to thanksgiuing for the benefit of our redēptiō.

4 That it might be a bond of mutuall loue and concord in the Church, that is to say, that by the partaking thereof we might more and more be bound amongst our selues in mutuall loue: for we that are many, are one bread and one body.

5 That it might be the bond of publicke meetings, & of the preseruing of the ecclesiasticall ministery. Exod. 12.16. 1. Cor. 11.20.

6 That it might be a note of our profession, whereby as by a cognisance, the Church is discerned frō infidels. Exo. 12.45. So by circūcisiō the Iews were discerned frō the Gētiles.

As all vncleane men were to be kept from eating the things offered to God, this threatning being added, that whatsoeuer vncleane man did eat of them, his soul should be cut off frō his people. Leu. 7.20. euen so no vncleane or vnbeleeuing man ought to vse the Sacrament of the couenant of Grace.

7 That it might be a witnesse of our confession and society with the church. The sixt end pertaineth to the whole Church: but the last end pertaineth to euery beleeuer.

He that shall not be circumcised, his soule shall be cut off frō the people of God. Whosoeuer vseth not the Sacraments whē he may, he sheweth that he is not a member of the Church, and the companion of our confession. For the Sacrament is a witnesse, which testifieth, that he who vseth the Sacraments doth pertaine to the company of the church, that he is a member of the Church, and that he hath fellowship with it. Whosoeuer in any congregation vseth the Sacrament, he by this vse doth testifie, that he embraceth the confession of that company, and that he hath fellowship with it.

<u>Thus farre concerning the ends of the couenant of grace.</u>

The Sacrament of the couenant of Grace is two fold: of the old Testament, or of the new.

The Sacrament of the old Testament, is that which before the cōming of Christ was instituted for the Church of the old Testament. Gen. 17. Exod. 12. & 16.15. & 17.6. 1. Cor. 10.1.2.3.4.

The Sacraments of the old Testamēt, were either ordinary, or extraordinary.

Ordinary Sacraments were those, which did ordinarily and alwayes pertaine to the Church of the old Testament. Genes. 17. Exod. 12.

And they were two: Circumcision, and the Passeouer.

Circumcision was a Sacrament of the old Testament, by which all the males amongst the people of Israell circumcised in the foreskin of their flesh, were ingraffed into the couenant that God made with Abraham. Gen. 17.10.11. Ios. 5.2. Rom. 4.11.

The parts thereof are two: the foreskin, and the outward action in the Circumcision. Genes. 17.11.

The foreskin, was a signe that our nature is corrupted, that men are borne guilty in this carnall generation: and therefore stand in neede of the regeneration and renewing which was to come by •he blessed seede, who should bruise the head of the serpent, and in whom all nations should be blessed.

The outward action in Circumcision was two fold: the one of the minister administring Circumcision, the other of a faithfull man receiuing Circumcision. Gen. 17.9.10. Rom. 2.19. & 4.11.

The action of the minister administring Circumcision was two fold: the laying open of the institution of Circumcision, and the Circumcision of the foreskin.

The Circumcision of the foreskin, was a signe of the Circumcision of the heart, that is to say, of iustification by faith, Rom. 4.11. of forgiuenesse of sinnes, and of regeneration, Deut. 30.6.

The action of a faithfull man receiuing Circumcision was two fold: the receiuing of circumcision, and thanksgiuing.

The receiuing of Circumcision, was that wherby a faithfull man, through the circumcision that was done by the hāds of the minister, did put off the foreskin of the flesh, to signifie, that he put off from him, the sinnes of the flesh. Col. 2.11. Rom. 4.11.

Thanksgiuing was done by the parents, and kinsfolkes, in stead of the infants being circumcised.

Thus farre concerning circumcision: now concerning the Passeouer.

The Passeouer was a Sacrament of the old Testament, whereby the faithfull hauing eaten the Paschall Lambe, were put in minde of their deliuerance out of Egypt, whether it were bodily already past, or spiruall and was to come. Exod. 12.1.2.3.5. & 11.

The parts of the Passeouer were two: the Paschall Lambe, and the action pertaining to the vse thereof

The Paschall Lambe by a spirituall signification, did note Christ the lambe of God, taking away the sinnes of the world. 1. Cor. 5.7.8. & 10.3.

The action in the Passeouer, was eyther of the minister, or of the receiuer.

The actiō of the Minister is two fold: both the laying open of the institution of the Sacrament of the Passeouer: and also the offering of it to men. Exod. 12.3.4.5.21.

The laying open of the institution of he Sacrament of the Passeouer is commanded. Exod. 12.26.27.

The offering of the Paschall Lambe to others, was made by the father of the family, and did signifie that God would giue his son, that he might be sacrificed for the sinnes of the world. 1. Cor. 5.7.

The action of the faithfull receiuer, was also two fold: the eating of the Paschall Lambe and thanksgiuing.

By the eating of the Paschall Lambe, was signified the participation of Christs passion. 1. Cor. 5.7.8.

In the thanksgiuing was remembred to the praise of God, the benefite of bringing forth the people of God from the bōdage of Egypt, as also the benefite of the deliuerance that should be from the spirituall Egypt, that is to say, from the bondage of sin, both which were to be wrought by the sacrifice of the Messias. Exod. 12.24.26. & 13.8.9.10.

Thus farre concerning the ordinary Sacraments of the old Testament: now concerning the extraordinary.

The extraordinary Sacraments, were those which were extrordinarily both before the instituting of the two ordinary Sacraments: as also those which were added to them afterward.

Before the ordinary Sacraments, were the sacrifices from Adam euen to Abraham. Genes. 4.4.

The extraordinary Sacraments which were added to the former two, were also two. The Baptisme of the cloud, and of the sea: and the supper of Manna, and of the water flowing out of the rocke.

The Baptisme of the cloud and sea, was an extraordinary Sacrament in the old Testament, whereby the Israelites being vnder that cloud, and passing through the sea, were all baptized into Moses, in that cloud and in that sea. 1. Cor. 10.1.2.

The supper of Māna & of the water flowing out of the rocke, was a Sacrament of the old Testament, whereby the Israelites were nourished with meat sent from heauen, to signifie the spirituall nourishment of the flesh of Christ, and did drinke the water flowing out of the rock, to signifie the spiritual drink of the bloud of Christ. 1. Cor. 10.3.4.

Hitherto concerning the Sacraments of the old Testament: now concerning the Sacraments of the new Testament.

A Sacrament of the new Testament, is that which being by Christ himselfe instituted for his owne Church, came in the roome of the Sacraments of the old Testament. Matt. 26.26. & 28.19.

The Sacraments of the new Testament are two: Baptisme, and the Lords supper.

Baptisme is a Sacrament of the new Testament, wherby is signified and sealed vp to vs, that we are as certainly washed in the bloud of Christ from sinnes, as our body is certainly washed through water in the name of the father, the sonne, and the holy Ghost. Mat. 28 19. Acts. 2.38. Mat. 3.11. Mark. 16.16. Rom. 6.3. Mar. 1.4. Luk. 3.3.

Baptisme commeth in the place of Circumcision, and kepeth the analogy and proportion thereof: for both of them is a Sacrament of entrance into the Church, and of regeneration.

And as the Israelites were but once circūcised: so we are but once baptized onely, because we are but once borne onely: and as circumcision was the first beginning of Iudaisme: so Baptisme is the first beginning of Christianity.

Of Baptisme there are two parts: the water of Baptisme, and the outward action in Baptisme.

By the water of Baptisme is signified, the bloud of Christ shed on the crosse. Heb. 12.24. 1. Pet. 1.1. Zach. 13.1. Ezec. 36.25.

The outward action in Baptisme is two fold: the one of the minister administring Baptisme: the other of a faithfull man vsing Baptisme. The action of the minister is two fold: the sanctification of the water, and the outward washing.

The sanctification of the water, is the appointing of it to this end, that it might signifie the bloud of Christ.

The outward washing is a signe, seale, and very sure pledge of the inward washing, whereby we with the bloud of Christ are washed from sins. Reue. 1.5. Rom. 6.3. 1. Cor. 1.6.11. 1. Pet. 3.21. Eph. 5.26. 1. Ioh. 1.7.

For as the filthinesses of the body are purged with water: so our sinnes are taken away by the bloud of Christ. Reue. 1.5. & 7.14. 1. Cor. 6.11. Gal. 3.17. 1. Ioh. 1.7.3.

Therefore the outward Baptisme is called the washing of regeneration. Tit. 3.5. The washing away of sinnes. Acts 22.16. not because the washing is properly and by it selfe that by which we are regenerated: for we are properly regenerated by the holy spirite: but because it is the signe and seale of the inward washing, that is to say, of regeneration and adoption according to the forme of the couenant; I will be thy God, and the God of thy seede. The minister washeth outwardly with water: but Christ washeth inwardly with his bloud. Mat. 3.11. Reue. 1.5.

<u>Thus farre concerning the action of the Minister administring Baptisme: now concerning the actions of a faithfull man receiuing Baptisme.</u>

The actions of a faithfull man vsing Baptisme is also two fold: the receiuing of Baptisme and thankesgiuing.

In the receiuing of Baptisme is signified, that the infant is by the bloud of Christ so certainely washed from sinnes, as his body is certainly sprinckled and washed with water. Reuel. 7.14. Ezech. 36.25.

To be washed with the bloud of Christ, is is to be made partakers of the benefites of the couenant of Grace, that is to say, to be reconciled, iustified, regenerated, adopted by God to be his sonnes, to be endued with the freedome of the sonnes of God, and so forth.

The outward man feeleth the force of the water: but the inward man feeleth the powerfull working of the bloud of Christ.

Euen Infidels are washed with water: but beleeuers onely with the bloud of Christ.

Therefore all who are Baptized, are not regenerated, but onely the beleeuers.

Now not onely those that are of yeares of discretiō are to be Baptized: but also infants.

- 1 Because they also do pertaine to the couenant of the grace of God.
- 2 Because to them also belōgeth the promise of forgiuenesse of sinnes through the bloud of Christ.
- 3 Because they belong to the Church of God.
- 4 Because they are redeemed by the bloud of Christ.
- 5 Because to them is promised the holy Spirite.
- 6 Because they are to be discerned from the children of Infidels.
- 7 Because also in the old Testament infants were circumcised.

Thankesgiuing is eyther presently done by the party Baptized, if he be of yeares of discretion: or else it is performed by the the witnesses in his stead if he bean infant: who yet when he commeth to ripe yeares, ought afterward in the whole course of his life to be thankefull to God for this benefite.

Hitherto concerning Baptisme: now concerning the Lords Supper.

The Lords Supper is a sacrament of the new Testament, by which is signified & sealed vp vnto vs, that we are as certainely nourished to eternall life by the body of Christ crucified, and by his bloud shed, as we do certainely with the mouth of our body eate the bread broken, and drinke the wine out of the cup. Mat. 26.26.27.28. Mark. 14.22.23.24. Luk. 22.19.20. 1. Cor. 10.16.17. &. 11.23.24.25. & 12.13.

In the fame sense it is called the table of the Lord. 1. Cor. 10.21.

Therefore thou doest come to the banket of Christ, thou art his guest, as oft as thou doest eat and drinke of this supper.

The Lords supper commeth in the roome of the Paschall Lambe: therefore it doth also keepe the analogie or proportion thereof. For both the one and the other is a Sacrament of nourishment and spirituall bringing vp.

And as the eating of the Paschall Lambe was often vsed: so also the vsing of the Lords Supper is oftentimes performed.

For as the Passeouer was the nourishing of Iudaisme: so the Lords Supper is the nourishing of Christianity, which nourishing often times standeth in neede of meat and drinke, that is to say, restoring and renewing, euen as our life doth daily want refreshing, which is performed by meat and drinke.

The parts of the Lords Supper, as of other sacraments, are two: the earthly matter, and outward action in the Supper.

The earthly matter in the Supper is two fold: the bread and the wine. Because we liue not only by meat, but by drinke also.

The bread in the holy Supper is a signe or image of Christs body giuen to death for vs. Ioh. 6.35.48.50.51.55.56.

The wine in the holy Supper is a signe or image of Christs bloud, shed on the crosse for vs.

Therefore the bread also is called the body it selfe, and the wine, or cup in which the wine is, is called the bloud it selfe.

Not that the body of Christ descendeth from the seate of his glory, out of heauen, and doth hide it selfe inuisibly in the bread, and his bloud in the wine, which opinion is most absurd: but therefore the bread is called the body of Christ, because it is a signe, remembrance, token, figure, similitude, and image of his body giuen for vs. And the wine or cup is called the new Testament or couenant, in the bloud of Christ: because it is a signe of the new Testament or couenaunt, that is to say, of reconciliation wrought with God, by the bloud of Christ shed vppon the Crosse for the forgiuenesse of sinnes. The bread by a metaphor, is called the body of Christ deliuered for vs, because the bread being broken, is a signe calling into our remembraunce, or imprinting in vs, and as it were setting before our eyes, the breaking, that is to say, the crucifying of the body of Christ. The wine by the same metaphor, is the bloud of Christ, because it is a signe calling into our remembrance, and imprinting in vs, the shedding of Christs bloud done on the crosse, for the forgiuenesse of our sinnes.

Yea the bread is not a signe of his glorious body, as it is now already glorified, but of his body deliuered vnto death, of his body broken on the crosse, and slayne for our sakes: as the Lord expresly sayth; This is my body which is giuen for you.

And the wine is not a signe of his bloud contayned in the veines, but of his bloud shed on the Crosse, or as it was shed: as the same Lord expresly testifieth.

And therefore the body of Christ is not now in the bread, because it is already glorious, and shall not before the last day descend from heauen vnto this miserable earth, neyther is his bloud already in the wine: because he once shed his bloud, and died, now he sheddeth it no more, death shall no more raigne ouer him.

By the bread being broken is represented vnto vs, as by a similitude, & a certaine image, his body that suffered for vs. For the whole action of the

Lords Supper is to be referred to this end, that we might preach the death of the Lord vntill he come.

The metaphor seemeth to be more conuenient in the laying open of these wordes, because not the bread simply, but the bread broken, by a certaine similitude, doth represent the body broken, as Paul sayeth: that is to say, deliuered vnto death. For the breaking of the bread, putteth vs in mind of the breaking of the body of Christ, as it were by a certaine picture set before our eyes. Christ did not simply call the bread his body, but the bread which is broken. But to what end? As I see with mine eyes that the bread is broken for me: so I am certainely confirmed in my faith, that the body of Christ was giuen vnto death for me. Secondly, as certainely as the minister of the word doth giue me the bread broken, so certainely doth Christ giue me his body deliuered to death for my sake.

That this is the naturall meaning of the words of Christ, by this it appeareth.

For Christ commaundeth to doe all these things in remembraunce of him, and Paul expoundeth that saying, yee shall preach the death of the Lord vntill he come.

Christ truely hath not said, the bread is the signe of my body: but because he ordayned the Sacrament, he speaketh of it as the Scripture is alwayes wont to speake concerning Sacraments, vnder a metaphor, calling the signe by the name of the thing signified.

And therefore the faithfull comming to the holy Supper, when they behold with the eyes of the body the Sacramentall bread, they are admonished, that withall, by the eyes of faith they behold and embrace the body of Christ, broken or crucified vppon the crosse for vs. For therefore the bread hath the name of the body, not that the faithfull should stand vppon the bread onely, or seeke the body of Christ in the earthly Element, but that they should by faith lift vp themselues into Heauen, whither he did ascend, and where he is, and by the eyes of faith should behold, and eate the vnspotted Lambe that was slaine for them on the heauēly Altar, the Church nameth it, saying; Lift vp your hearts.

By the same metaphor the bread which we breake, is by Paul called the communion of the body of Christ, the cuppe of blessing which we blesse is called the communion of the bloud of Christ. 1. Cor. 10.16. Because by this bread and cup, as by a seale, the faithfull are assured that they haue communion, that is to say, fellowship with Christ.

Both the matters, that is to say, the earthly and heauenly, are indeede present in the holy Supper: the former indeede bodily and visibly, but the other spiritually, & by the sight which faith affordeth vs.

We with the eyes of the body see the bread and wine: but with the eyes of the soule, that is to say, with faith, we see the body and bloud of Christ.

Therefore as certainely as we see the bread and wine to be present: so certainely doe we beleeue that the body and bloud of Christ is present to vs: yea we doe not beleeue that it is the Lords supper, except his body & bloud be present to vs.

Otherwise if they were absent, how could it be made the partaking of the body and bloud of Christ, for the partaking is not of things that are absent, but present.

But the body and bloud of Christ, are truly present to the faithfull, that is to say, to those who receiue it by faith, and yet this is by a spirituall presence, not by a locall, or bodily presence or placing: by a Sacramental presence, and such as belongeth to a couenant not by a naturall presence: the body & bloud of Christ are present, by such a kinde of presence as faith requireth & would haue, not as the bodily mouth: such a one as the spirit requireth and not the letter: such a one as the purpose of Christ calleth for, & not a Capernaiticall interpretation: and therefore rather we should by our minde be caried vp into heauen, then to haue the blessed and glorious flesh of our Lord Iesus Christ pulled out of heauen vpon this miserable earth, & to imagine his inuisible descending into the bread, and againe his ascending into heauen, after the holy supper is celebrated.

<u>Hitherto concerning the earthly matter in the holy Supper: now concerning the outward action.</u>

The outward action in the Lordes supper, as in other Sacraments, is two fold: one of the minister that administreth the Lords supper, and another of a faithfull man vsing the holy supper.

The action of the minister that administreth the holy supper is two fold: the sanctifying of the bread and wine, and the administring of it.

The sanctifying of the bread and wine is an action of the minister, whereby according to the commandemēt of Christ, he ordaineth the bread and wine to a holy vse.

The reciting of the words of the institutiō and promise, is done for the blessing of the bread and wine, that is to say, that of the cōmon bread & wine they might be made holy signes of the body & bloud of Christ. Which consecrating, sanctifying and appointing of the bread and wine to a holy vse, was called of old writers, a change, that is to say, such a chaunging as belongeth to Sacraments.

Which chaunging of the earthly matter, is not a change of the substāce, as the Papists erroniously affirme, but a change of the end: because the bread & wine are no more common meat and drinke, but serue to a holy end and vse.

For the mysticall signes, euen after sanctifying doe not loose their owne nature: Paul after the blessing, calleth the bread still bread.

The administring of the earthly matter, is the other part of the ministers actiō, wherby he administreth the earthly matter in the holy supper.

And that administring is two fold, partly of the bread, partly of the wine.

Of the administring of the bread there are two parts, the breaking and the distributing.

The breaking of the bread is an action of the minister, whereby is signified that the bodie of Christ was no lesse certainely offered and broken on the crosse for me, then I with my eyes see the bread of the Lord broken for me.

The distributing of the bread, is an action of the minister, whereby is signified that the body of Christ is as certainely offered to me, as the bread broken is certainely offered to me.

Of the administring of the wine there are also two parts: the powring of the wine into the cup, and the distributing of the cup.

The powring out of the wine, is an action of the minister, whereby is signified the shedding of the bloud of Christ, done on the crosse.

The distributing of the cup is an action of the minister, whereby is signifyed that the bloud of Christ is as certainely giuen vs, as the cup is certainely deliuered vnto vs.

Thus farre concerning the action of the minister: now concerning the outward action of a faithfull man vsing the holy Supper.

The outward action of a faithfull man vsing the holy supper is two folde: the receiuing of the bread and wine, and thankesgiuing.

The receiuing of the bread and wine, is an action of a faithfull man vsing the holy supper, wherby he eateth the bread and drinketh the wine, to signifie that he doth as certainely by faith eate the body of Christ and drinke his bloud, as hee doth certainely with the mouth of the body eate the bread and drinke the wine out of the cup.

To eate the body of Christ, is to be made a partaker of the benefites of the couenant of grace, that is to say, of reconciliation, iustification, and regeneration in Christ, of adoption, &c.

Abraham did eate the flesh of Christ, before that by his owne substance he had any being in his manhood. We eate the flesh of Christ, no otherwise then Abraham did: neither are wee made partakers of the flesh of Christ otherwise then Abraham was. Ioh. 6.51. 1. Cor. 10.16. This eating is onely spirituall, because it is done by faith and the spirite. Whereby it appeareth, that the beleeuers only doe eate the body and drinke the bloud of Christ: the reprobate doe not, because they haue no faith.

Now the flesh of Christ in that respect only that it was slaine and dead for vs, is eaten to quicken the godly: & the bloud of Christ, onely as it was shed on the crosse, is drunke for the forgiuenesse of our sinnes.

For although Christ being once dead, and raysed from the dead, dyeth not anie more, and so is not now any more in the state of humiliation, but of glory, yet the Sacraments leade our faith to the sacrifice of Christ, performed on the crosse, as Christ sayth: Doe this in remembrance of me, and Paul sayth, As oft as you shall eate of this bread, and drinke of this cuppe, yee shall preach the death of the Lord vntill he come.

Hitherto concerning the receiuing of the bread and wine: now concerning thankesgiuing.

Thankesgiuing is an action of a faithfull mā vsing the holy supper, by which through true faith he thinketh & speaketh of Christs death to his praise. 1. Cor. 11.26.

Thus farre concerning the parts of the Lordes Supper: now concerning the preparation of a faithfull man before the vse thereof.

The preparation to the vse of the holy Supper is two fold: inward and outward.

The inward preparation is spiritual, which consisteth in a mans examining of himselfe, or in trying his owne worthinesse or vnworthinesse.

The worthinesse and vnworthinesse of those who come to the holy Supper, and the effects of them both are two folde: either of the person or of the vsing.

The worthines of the person is faith, or the righteousnesse of Christ imputed by fayth, which whosoeuer hath, they are worthy guests, & receiue this food to eternal saluatiō.

Therfore the worthines of the person cōsisteth in faith alone, and the effect of it is the escaping of eternall punishment.

The vnworthines of a person is infidelity, wherewith whosoeuer are possessed, they are vnworthy of this table, and receiue to themselues iudgement and eternall damnation.

The worthinesse of the vsing is true reuerence, inward and outward, forgiuenes, loue, a serious bewayling of sinnes repentance, the meditation of the benefites of Christ, the discerning of the body of the Lord, thankesgiuing, the auoyding of all offences.

Nowe the worthinesse hath place in the faithfull onely.

The vnworthines of the vsing, is the vnreuerent or irreligious offering of the Lords Supper.

The same indeede is alwaies in persons which are vnworthy, yet sometime euen in the worthy partakers.

And therefore it is two folde: one in the wicked, the other in the godly.

The vnworthines of the vsing in the wicked, is a want & absence of true reuerence, inward & outward, of forgiuenes, of loue, of a serious bewailing of sins, & of repentance, of the meditation of the benefites of Christ, of thankesgiuing, of the discerning of the body of the Lord, & of the auoiding of all offences.

The vnworthines of the vsing in the godly, is a negligence and colder feeling in the trying of himselfe.

For although the godly doe indeede eate the bread of the Lorde, and the bread which is the Lorde, and therefore eate eternall saluation, free from eternall iudgement, yet they comming vnreuerently to the Lordes Table, that is to say, trying themselues too negligently and coldly, doe eate to thēselues temporall iudgement, that is to say, they offend God, and are by diuers chastisements in this life called backe to the amending of these sinnes. So Paul doth with a threatning of temporall punishment terrifie the Corinthians, comming vnreuerently to the Lords Table, although some of them notwithstanding being truely conuerted: and yet neuerthelesse he rayseth them vp againe with consolation. 1. Cor. 11.30.31.32.

For euen the faithfull do oftentimes sinne by this kind of negligence and carelessenesse: and although their eternall saluation be not made frustrate, yet they are hardly chastened in this life. The Apostle teacheth this plainely, when the Corinthians sinning in the irreligious vsing of the Lords Supper, whether by affections or by ignorance, doth yet call them brethren, and doth say that they are punished of the Lord with diseases, and temporall death for this fault, that they might not be condemned with this world. 1. Cor. 11.30.31.32. as 1. Cor. 3.12. hee sayth; Those which build haye and stubble on that foundation, which is Christ, they shall indeede be saued, but yet as it were by fire.

In all the faithfull indeede there is some parcel of this vnworthines, but in some more, in some lesse: and those who haue care to auoyde it, & keepe a good conscience, are pardoned for Christs sake.

And therefore there is required a tryall of both these sorts of worthines: that wee may escape not onely the eternall, but the temporary wrath and punishment of God. 1. Cor. 11.28.

Concerning the trying of a mans selfe before the vse of the Supper of the Lord.

The trying or examining of a mans selfe consisteth in two things: first whether thou be in the faith, whether thou vnderstand the articles of fayth, the promise of the Gospell, and doctrine of the Sacraments. In this case the Creede of the Apostles, or doctrine of the Gospell is the touchstone. Here is to be taken from the people that opinion wherwith many are possessed, who (these three words being taken hold of, THIS IS MY BODY) suppose that it is not necessarie to search more diligently the nature of the Sacraments they wil beleeue simply: but this is not to beleeue, but to erre, and indeed to erre obstinately, if thou hast purposed that thou wilt not learne any thing. If thou wilt rightly beleeue, it behooueth thee to haue vnderstanding: for faith is a sure knowledge. For what fruite shall they receiue by the vse of the Sacramēts, vvho neuer haue rightly learned the vse of them?

The other part consisteth in examining ones life. In this case the ten commandements is a touchstone, that is to say, wee must trye how we haue led our life, how farre it is from the lawe of God, what it ought to be: whether thou hast performed those things which thou hast promised to God in baptisme: whether thou loue God aboue all things, and thy neighbour as thy selfe, that is to say, whether thou doest, and hereafter wilt doe those thinges which God commaundeth: and whether thou eschewest and wilt eschewe those thinges which God forbiddeth: whether thou hast a setled purpose to amende thy life, and to frame the same according to the worde of God. If there be any who feele such an inclination in themselues, they are to be exhorted to goe to the holy Supper; the rest, who neither vnderstand the doctrine of the promise of the Gospell and Sacraments: neither desire to amend their life, but haue a mind to continue in their faultes, they are to be disswaded, not to goe to the hol• Supper, least they eate iudgement to themselues.

<u>Hitherto concerning the Sacrament of the eternall couenant: now concerning the Sacrament of the temporall couenant.</u>

The Sacrament of the temporal couenant, is a Sacrament whereby God confirmeth the bodily promise: such as is the rainebow. Gen. 8.12.13. Such as was the fleece of Gedeon. Iud. 6.36. euen to the end. Also the going backe, both of the shadow in the dyall of Ahaz, as also of the Sunne, when God promised to king Hezekiah, the deliuerance of the citie from Senacherib, and the adding of fifteene yeares to the space of his life. Esa. 38.5.6.7.8.

<u>Thus farre concerning the workes of God which are done in this life: now concerning those workes which shall be done in the life to come.</u>

The workes of God which shall be done after this life, are both the generall raysing vp of the dead, and the last iudgement: and also the manifesting of Gods glory to all eternitie.

The generall raysing vp of the dead, is a worke of God by which after the number of the elect shall be fulfilled, he will call all men being dead to life againe. Act. 3.24. 1. Pet. 3.7. Reuel. 6.11.

The last iudgement, is that wherby Christ will declare all without exception, being iudged by his word, some to be heires of eternall life, some to be partakers of eternall fire with the deuill. Matth. 25.31. Rom. 14.10. 2. Cor. 5.10.

The godly haue this comfort of the last iudgement, that the father hath deliuered all iudgement to the sonne, that hee might giue peace to our consciences, and might take away all feare of condemnation. Ioh. 5.

Of the last iudgement there are two parts: the separation of the elect from the reprobate, and the finall sentence.

The separation of the elect from the reprobate, is that wherby all men being gathered from all the corners of the world by the Angels, the elect shalbe set at the right hand, and the rebrobate at the left hand of Christ. Matth. 25.33.

The finall sentence is the other part of the last iudgement, whereby Christ shall minister iustice to euery one, and shall render to euery one according to his workes. Matth. 25.32.33. Rom. 1.6.1. Corinth. 4.5. Reuel. 20.12.15.

The finall sentence shall be two fold: the one pronounced to the elect, and the other denounced against the reprobate.

The finall sentence pronounced to the elect, is this: Come yee blessed of my father, and possesse ye the kingdome prepared for you before the foūdations of the world were laid. Matth. 25.34.

Of the finall sentence pronounced to the elect there are two parts: the one concerning the bringing of the elect of the possession of the eternall inheritance and blessednesse, the other concerning their glorification.

The glorification of the elect is a worke of God, whereby he shall with eternall glory adorne all the elect, after the generall resurrection of the dead.

This glorification pertaineth both to the body, and to the soule.

The glorification pertaining to the bodie, is in that it shall be made spirituall, that is to say, because it shall leade a spirituall life, free, and deliuered from all the spot of the flesh, such a one as the spirits themselues do leade: furthermore incorruptible, immortall, lastly conformable to the glorious body of Christ. For the bodyes of the godly, shall not only be immortall and incorruptible, but also strong, impassible, glorious, spirituall. 1. Corinth. 15.

Augustine to Crescentius; As the naturall body is not a soule but a body, so wee ought not to call the spirituall body, a spirit, but a body.

It is of Paul called the spirituall body: then not a spirite, for the spirite hath not a bodie, that is to say, flesh & bones. Therfore the spirite and the spirituall body are not one. And Paul doth not say that the substāce of the body shalbe changed in the resurrection, but the qualities of the body and substance: for so he writeth to the Corinthians, that this body which is subiect to corruption, may put on an incorruptible nature, & the mortall may put on immortality. But (sayest thou) it shall not haue a matter subiect to perishing. Who denieth it? Yet it shall not want a matter. Hath not euen the heauē an impassible matter void of corruption? You except: but we shall be like the Angels; then we shall not be Angels: for our flesh must rise againe, and we in the same (as Iob sayth) shall see God our Sauiour. If our bodies shall be changed into spirites: then man shall not rise againe, because man consisteth of bodie and soule, and the bodie cannot passe into the spirite, for they do not agree in matter. By Paul a spirituall body is opposed to a naturall body, but vnderstande by a naturall body, a changeable and weake bodie: for our bodie ceaseth not to be a naturall body, although it be made immortall and impassible; for euen the heauen is a naturall body, which yet cōsisteth of a nature not passible nor vanishing.

The glorification pertayning to the soule, shalbe an enlightening of the soule, with the full knowledge of the mysteries of God, and with an vnchangeable vprightnes of the will.

<u>Thus farre concerning the finall sentence to be pronounced to the elect: now concerning the finall sentence to be denounced against the reprobate.</u>

The sentence to be denounced against the rebrobate, is this: Goe ye cursed into the euerlasting fire, which is prepared for the deuill and his Angels.

<u>Hitherto concerning the generall raysing vp of the dead, and the last iudgement: now concerning the manifestation of the glory of God to all eternitie.</u>

The manifestation of the glory of God to all eternitie, shal thē be after that Christ shal deliuer the kingdome to God his father, and Christ himselfe shall also in respect of his humanitie, subiect himselfe to God his father, that God the father may be all in all thinges. 1. Cor. 15.24.28. Eph. 2.7.

Hitherto we haue layd open faith concerning God: now concerning the Church.

> The Church is a companie of men professing a certaine religion.
> Religion is a forme of worshipping God.
> The Church is two fold, true or false.
> The true Church, is a company of men professing the true religion.
> The true religion, is that whereby the true God is rightly worshipped.
> And that is onely one.
> And in that alone men shall be saued.
> But the true Church is vniuersall or particular; this latter is visible, the other inuisible.
> The vniuersal Church is an inuisible company of the elect only, to eternal saluation. Matth. 8.11. Ioh. 10.16. Gal. 4.26.
> And that is also called the kingdome of Christ or of God in the Lords prayer, in the Prophets it is called the kingdome of the Messias. Also a Lot. Ephes. 1.11. The lot or inheritance of the Lord, to which not onely the Priestes, but also the vnlearned pertaine.
> And that is called vniuersall.
> - 1 Because it is the generall company of the elect. who altogether make one misticall body
> - 2 Because all that beleeue in God, and are to be saued, must be in this company: for without the church there is no saluation.
> - 3 Because it comprehēdeth the whole body of the doctrine of the Prophetes and Apostles.
> - 4 Because it is dispersed through the whole face of the earth. Esa. 2.2.3.
>
> And it is onely one. Ephes. 2.14.15.16.17.
> The head of the vniuersal Church is Christ Iesus alone. 1. Cor. 12.27. Ephes. 1.22. & 4.15. & 5.23. Col. 1.18. & 2.10.
> And he hath no neede of a Vicar, nor of a ministeriall head.
> But the body of the vniuersall Church is misticall. Rom. 12.5. 1. Cor. 10.17. & 12.27. Eph. 1.22.23. & 4.4.12.16. & 5.23. Col. 1.15.24.
> The members thereof are onely the elect. 1. Ioh. 2.19. Ioh. 10.14.27.28.
> And these members are both of the Iewes, and also of the Gentiles.
> And both these members are eyther in heauen, or on earth. Eph. 1.10.
> They are in heauen, who are already departed in the faith of Christ.
> They are on earth, who beleeue in Christ and yet liue.

Thus farre concerning the vniuersall Church, now concerning the particular.

The particular Church, is a visible cōpany of men in any place whatsoeuer, who heare the sincere word of God, and rightly vse the Sacraments, among whom are many euill hypocrites, and vnbeleeuers mingled, and so shall be to the last day. Mat. 13.24.47.

Now that it is the true Church of Christ, the essētiall notes of the true church do shew.

The essentiall notes of the true Church, are properties by which it may be vnfallibly knowen, which particular company being any where gathered together, is the true Church of God.

And these notes are two: the sincere preaching of Gods word, and the right vse of the Sacraments.

The sincere preaching of Gods word, is that, when according to the forme of wholesome words, all things necessary to eternall saluation, are out of the word of God onely taught to the edifying of the Church. Ioh. 8.31.47. 2. Ioh. 1.9. Ioh. 10.27. & 14.23. Act. 2.42. 2. Pet. 1.19. Eph. 1.20. Gal. 1.8.9. 1. Cor. 3.11. Mat. 28.20. Rom. 10.8. Act. 17.11.

The right vse of the Sacraments is that, when the Sacraments are administred, and receiued according to the institution of Christ. Mar. 16.6. Act. 2.38. & 10.47. Luk. 22.19. Act. 2.42.

The particular Church, is either of the old Testament, or of the new. Eph. 2.17.

The Church of the old Testamēt was that which was among the people of God, before the comming of Christ. Eph. 2.11.12.

The Church of the new Testament is that, which began after the comming of Christ. Eph. 2.13.14. There is a certaine setled gouernment of them both.

The Ecclesiasticall gouernment, is a well ordered state of the Church, or else it is an order consisting of certaine lawes according to the word of God, and the same tending to the preseruing of the well ordered estate of the Church. 1. Cor. 1.10. & 14.40. Col. 2.5.

And that gouernment is either proper or common.

The proper gouernment is that, which belōgeth to the office of seuerall persōs, who are in the church. Mat. 18.17.18. Rom. 12.6.7.8.

Those persons are either ministers or hearers.

Ministers are those, who hauing a lawfull calling, are set ouer the Church. Rom. 12.6.7.8. 2. Cor. 2.6.

And they are either ordinary or extraordinary. 1. Cor. 12.28.29.31. The office of the former is perpetuall in the Church, the other but temporary.

Ordinary ministers are those, who do employ their ordinary labor on the church, both by an ordinary maner, and also endued with ordinary gifts. Rom. 12.6. 1. Cor. 12.4.

Extraordinary ministers are those, who are raised vp besides order, either to lay the foundations of Churches, or to restore them being broken downe, or to amend them that are decayed. 1. Cor. 12.28.29. Eph. 4.11.

Those that were called extraordinarily had this testimony, that they could not erre in doctrine, because God did testifie concerning it. Yet in life and manners, both they might sin, and sometime also haue sinned. Gal. 2.14.

Ministers that were extraordinarily called, had extraordinary gifts, namely, extraordinary prophecies, and the giftes of working miracles. 1. Cor. 12.9.10.

An extraordinary prophecy was that, by which through the singular gift of God, they were enabled both to interpret and apply Scriptures: and also most surely and clearely to foretell things to come. Ioh. 10.8.12.

The gift of working miracles was that, whereby they did seale vp their prophecy, and doctrine.

The ministry of the Church of the old Testament ordinarily called, were Priests and Leuites.

Priests were those, to whom oldinarily the administring of the true worship of God in the church of the old Testament was committed. Exod 28.41. & 29.1.

Leuites were those, who were appointed to looke to the tabernacle, and to all thinges which appertained to it. Num. 1.50. & 3.6. Deut. 10.8.

The Prophets in the old Testament, were those who were sent by an extraordinary calling, both to the restoring of the doctrine corrupted by the Priests, & also to prophecy of the Messias, and of other things to come, and also to the gouerning of certain politick counsels. 1. Sam. 9.9. 2. Chron. 9.29. Esa. 1.1. Ier. 1.3. Ose. 1.1. Amo. 1.1. Aba. 1.1.

<u>Hitherto concerning the Ministers of the church of the old Testament: now concerning the Ministers of the Church of the new Testament.</u>

The Ministers of the Church of the new Testament, who were extraordinarily called, were Iohn Baptist, the Apostles, and Euangelists, and Prophets of the new Testament. Ioh. 1.6. 7. Eph. 4.11. 1. Cor. 12.28.

Te office of these ministers was temporary, being instituted particularly for that time, in which at the beginning, the Churches of the new Testament were to be planted. Mat. 28.19.

Iohn Baptist was the sonne of the Priest Zachariah, and Elizabeth, ordained by God, to be the forerunner of the Messias, & to prepare the way for him. Luk. 2.

The Apostles were teachers immediatly appointed by Christ himselfe, to preach the Gospell euery where throughout the whole world. Mat. 28.19.

The Euāgelists were those, who were next the Apostles in office. And sometime did supply their places.

And some of them were Apostles, as Mathew and Iohn: for the same person might vndergo like offices: and certaine of them were the companions and fellow labourers of the Apostles, as Marke and Luke.

And because the Church of the new Testament was to be gathered out of al nations, therefore chiefly the Apostles and Euangelists were indued with the gift of tongues. Act. 2.4.

The Prophets of the new Testamēt were those, who being endued with some singular reuealing of the misteries of God, foretold things to come, as for example Agabus. Act. 11.27. & 21.10. and Iohn in the Reuelation. Paul also in the Rom. 11.25. speaking concerning the restoring of the Iewes. & 2. Thess. 2.3. concerning Antichrist.

<u>Hitherto concerning the extraordinarie Ministers of the Church of the new Testament: now concerning the ordinary.</u>

The ministers of the Church of the new Testament ordinarily called, are either Bishops or their helpers. Eph. 4.11.

The office of these men is perpetuall, that is to say, which is required in the Church euen to the end of the world.

Bishops are those, who are occupied about spirituall things, and such as pertaine vnto God.

The office of a Bishop therefore, is an Ecclesiasticall office, which is occupied in heauenly things, and such as pertaine to God. 1. Tim. 3.1.2.

Bishops are Pastors or Doctors. Ephes. 4.11.

Pastors are those who are set ouer the church, according to the commandement of Christ.

And they are also called Elders.

Of the office of the Pastor there are two parts: the ecclesiasticall ministery, and the ecclesiasticall power.

The ecclesiasticall ministery is the first part of the office of a Pastor, consisting in teaching the word of God, and administring of the Sacraments, to the vndoubted profite of the church.

Of the ecclesiasticall ministery there are two parts: the application of the word to the vses of the church, and administration of the Sacraments.

The application of the word to the vses of the Church, is the first part of the ecclesiastical ministery, which is exercised in teaching, comforting, rooting out of false opinions, exhorting, correcting, and so forth. And that both publickly in the cōgregatiō of the people: and also priuatly, specially if any be pressed with diseases, or other calamity, or molested with the temptations of Sathan.

The administration of the Sacraments, is the other part of the ecclesiasticall ministery, when the Pastors according to the institution of Christ, administer the Sacraments.

Thus farre concerning the Ecclesiasticall ministery: now concerning the Ecclesiasticall power.

The ecclesiasticall power, is the other part of the Pastors office, whereby the authority of the church is preserued,

The ecclesiasticall power is two fold: of order and iurisdiction.

The power of order, is a power to set order in the ecclesiasticall gouernment.

And it is either in the lawfull calling of ministers: or in making ecclesiasticall lawes.

The lawfull calling of ministers is that, when according to the word of God, fit persons are chosen to the office of teaching, and admininstring the Sacraments.

The parts thereof are two: examination, and ordination.

The examination is two fold: of doctrine and of life.

The examinatiō of doctrine, is an examining whereby triall is made, whether the person to be chosen be able to teach the Church: For bow shall he teach others that, which he hath not learned himselfe? 2. Tim. 2.2. Tit. 1.9.

The examination of life is an examining whereby triall is made whether the person to be chosen, hath honest & vnblameable manners. Tit. 1.6.7.8.9.

Ordination is an appointing of the examined person to vndergo some office.

The Ecclesiasticall Lawes, are rules according to which, the Ecclesiasticall gouernmēt ought to be administred.

Hitherto concerning the power of order: now concerning the power of Iurisdiction.

The power of Iurisdiction, is a power to exercise the ecclesiasticall iudgementes.

And it is either in the censure, or in the power of the keyes.

The censure is that, whereby escapes, either in doctrine or manners, hauing beene obserued in some, they are corrected, and that either by priuate admonition, or by taking one or two witnesses, that so in al parts of his office, he may do those things which are prescribed in the word of God. Mat. 18.11.16.

The power of the keyes, is an Ecclesiasticall power, whereby heauen is opened to the beleeuers, but shut to vnbeleeuers. Ioh. 20.21.22.23. Mat. 16.19. & 18.18.

The partes thereof are two, loosing or binding.

The loosing is a part of the power of the keyes, when to those that repent, forgiuenes of sinnes, and the grace of God is preached.

The binding is the other part of the power of the keyes, when the wrath of God is denounced to the impenitent.

This power of the keyes is exercised, either by preaching the word, or by ecclesiasticall discipline.

The power of the keyes by preaching of the word, is when the ministers of the word do preach and testifie to all euery one that repēteth, & taketh hold of Christ by faith· that God hath pardoned all their sins by the merite of Christ. But contrariwise they denoūce to the impenitent, vnbeleuers and hypocrites, that the wrath of God and eternall condemnation doth hang ouer them, as long as they continue in their sinnes: according to which testimony of the Gospell, God shall iudge in this life and in the life to come.

The Ecclesiasticall discipline is a spirituall execution of the ecclesiasticall lawes.

Of that there are two parts: the ecclesiasticall punishment, and the absoluing from the punishment.

The Ecclesiastical punishmēt is that, which in the Church is layed on them that sinne.

And that is lighter or greater.

The lighter punishmēt is a rebuking, when he is reprooued who hath sinned, either by ignorance, or priuatly without the offence of others.

A greater Ecclesiasticall punishment is that, which is layed on him who hath sinned more grieuously, namely both of meere malice, and also with the offence of others.

And that is two fold: suspension or excommunication.

Suspension is an ecclesiasticall punishmēt, whereby the offender is not for a certain time admitted, either to the vse of the holy supper, or to the rest of the holy things of the church.

Excommunication is an ecclesiasticall punishment, whereby a lawfull knowledge going before, he who hath contemned the former priuate or ecclesiasticall admonitions, is declared to be excluded iustly from the company of the Church and kingdome of God, and to be deliuered to Sathan, except he repent. Mat. 18.17. 1. Cor. 5.3. 1. Tim. 1.20.

And excommunication is done, either for dāgerous errors about the foundations of religiō, which any mā doth obstinatly defend, and raiseth in the church scismes, & heresies, and doth stubburnly and seditiously trouble the peace of the church▪ 1. Tim. 1.20. Tit. 3.10.

Or for manifest faults, which tend to the offence and slander of the Church. 1. Cor. 5.3.

The ends of excommunication are two.

The first is this, that by this remedy the flesh of the excommunicat might be tamed, that he might learne to liue to the spirit, that is to say, that the excommunicate ouercome with shamefastnes, might be stirred vp to repentance, and decline from euill. 1. Cor. 5.5.2. Cor. 2.7, 2. Thess. 3.14. 1. Tim. 1.20.

The other, that contagion might not come to the rest, and infect them also. 1. Cor. 5.6.7.

Thus farre concerning the Ecclesiasticall punishment: now concerning absolution.

Absolution is a freeing from the punishment, after repentance is sufficiently testified.

And that is either priuate or publicke.

Priuat is that, by which either those that were rebuked or suspended are absoled. Mat. 18.15.

Publicke is that, by which the excommunicate after repentance sufficiently testified publickly, are reconciled to the Church, and are receiued againe into the society thereof. 2. Cor. 2.6.10.

Hitherto concerning Pastors: now concerning Doctors.

Doctors are those who onely giue themselues to the interpretation of the Scripture, either in turning it into other tongues, or in searching out the true sense of it, that so sincere and wholesome doctrine may be retained among the faithfull.

Therefore the office of Doctors is occupied in a scholer-like and exquisite interpretation of the word of God. Rō. 12.5. 1. Co. 1.12.8.

Thus farre concerning Bishops: now concerning their helpers.

The helpers of Bishops are those, who are adioyned to the Bishops for the Ecclesiasticall businesses.

And they are either gouernours or disposers of the Church goods.

The gouernours are graue and godly men chosen out of the people, who together with the Bishops are set ouer the cēsure of maners, and of exercising discipline. Rom. 12.7. 1. Cor. 12. These by a Sinecdoche, of the generall for the speciall, are called Elders.

Their company is called the eldership.

Hitherto concerning the gouernours: now concerning the disposers of the Church goods.

The disposers of the church goods, are such helpers of Bishops as dispose bodily things.

And they are Deacons, or Deaconesses.

Deacons are those, who dispose the goods of the Church.

The goods of the Church are diuided into foure parts.

One part is distributed to them who are appointed for the ministery of the Church. Mat. 10.10. 1. Cor 9.9. 1. Thess. 3.8.

The other fourth part, is bestowed in the maintaining of the poore.

The third part is appointed for the vpholding the building of churches.

The fourth part that remaineth, is appointed to the Bishop, to the end that he may entertaine poore strangers and helpe also the captiue brethren when it is needefull. 1. Tim. 3.2. Tit. 1.8.

But yet now a dayes, those are also called Deacons, that are adioyned to the Pastors to helpe them, in teaching in preaching, in administring the Sacraments, in visiting the sicke and captiue, and in other things pertaining to the holy ministery.

Thus farre concerning Deacons: now concerning Deaconesses.

Deaconesses are widowes, who serue to the vses of the poore and sicke. Act. 6.11. Tim. 5.9.

Hitherto concerning the Ministers of the church: now concerning the hearers.

The hearers are all the rest of the saints in the Church besides the ministers, whose duty is willingly to submit themselues to the ecclesiasticall discipline, and to further it according to their ability, with gifts, labour, and by what meanes soeuer they can Heb. 13.17. 1. Tim. 5.17.18. Otherwise they are called ley men, priuate men.

Thus farre concerning the proper gouernment of the church: now concerning the common.

The common gouernment of the Church, is that, which doth pertaine to all the members of the whole body of the Church.

And that appeareth in the ecclesiasticall counsels: for euery one may and ought to be heard in them, so that it be done duely and in order.

The ecclesiasticall counsell, is an assembly instituted for the causes of the Church.

Otherwise it is called a Synode.

But the cause of calling together of counsels: is two fold.

One that the Church may defend the sincere doctrine comprehended in the word of God against hereticks, and approoue it by open testimony. Act. 15.

In this regard the Church is called the piller, or ground of truth, to wit, whereof it is a faithfull witnesse 1. Tim. 3.15.

The other, that it might appoint lawes or rules of the ecclesiastical gouernment, according to the diuers respects, of times, places and persons.

The counsell is generall or particular.

Generall is that, which is gathered in the name of the whole Church: as was that of the Israelites. 1. King. 18.19. and of the Apostles. Act. 15.6.

The particular counsell is that, which is gathered in the name of some certaine church.

And that is called prouinciall or nationall, when the chosen ministers of the church of one prouince or nation meete together.

The Synod of some choise of learned and godly men, is to be gathered together by the authority of the magistrate.

We must not make any decree concerning the order and manner of conferring with the aduersaries, except the magistrate be present, or else men chosen by the magistrate.

The order must be according to method. The positions must be definitions, distributions, short axiomes. The manner of disputing must be alwayes by syllogismes.

But all things that are done by writing, are to be subscribed with the very hand of those who are to confer: or if they do rather choose to deale by speach, the sayings of both parties are to be written by approoued notaries of good credit, and chosen by the consent of either partie, which afterward both parties may ouersee, and confirme it by adding the subscription. For this truly is the iust and sincere forme of conference, that so falsehood may be preuented.

The positions of the conference which are propounded must be vndoubted, and very few also: let not liberty be giuen to wander from them: neyther yet are all the iudgements and interpretations of priuate men to be defended, but euery part must clearely propound and defend his owne iudgement: for it is neither needefull nor necessary, that all the iudgements and sayings of all men be approued by vs. For why should we defend the particular iudgement and authority of other men, if we our selues be of another minde.

The controuersies after both parties heard are finally to be determined. From which determination & deciding, the ciuil magistrats are not to be excluded, but admitted to it. For both Zenas the Lawyer is highly commended by Paul, and ioyned with Apollo as equall with him. Tit. 3.13.

Hitherto concerning the true church: now concerning the false Church.

The false Church is that which followeth a false religion.
A false religion, is what religion soeuer is contrarie to the word of God, deliuered in the holy Scripture.
Whosoeuer embrace this, are the enemies of Christ, and his kingdome, or true Church.
The enemies are either open or dissembled.
The open enemies are those, who do manifestly shew thēselues enemies to the name of Christians.
And they are both blasphemous Iewes, and Gentiles.
The blasphemous Iewes, are the open enemies of the christian religion who though Iesus Christ the promised Messias be already manifested, yet looke for an other and speake euil of the Lord Iesus and his mēbers, neither will they beleeue the Gospell concerning Iesus Christ.
In them especially we must consider both their reiection and also restoring.
The reiection of the Iewes, is a most iust punishment which by God is layd vpon thē, whilest he hath blinded and hardened them being vnthankefull towardes Christ and his Gospell, and reiected them from his couenant, that he might call and adopt the Gentiles in their stead. Act. 13.46. Rom. 11. chap. almost throughout.
And that is neither generall nor perpetuall. Rom. 11.
The restoring of the Iewes is a benefite of God, when God after that the fulnesse of the Gentiles is come in into the Church, shall conuert the Iewes, that they being kindled with an emulation of the mercy shewed to yᵉ Gentiles, might embrace that Gospell which concerneth Christ, and be ingraffed againe into the couenant of Grace made with Abraham and their fathers, and might be saued. Rom. 11.23.24.25.26.27.28.29.30.31.32.

Hitherto concerning the Iewes: now concerning the Gentiles.

The Gentiles are open enemies to the Christian religion, who worshippe false and counterfeit Gods.

And they be either Mahumets or other Pagans.

Mahumets are open enemies to the Christian religion, who worship Mahumet, and embrace the Alcoran deliuered vnto them by him. They are also called Turkes.

Other Pagans are also besides the Mahumets, which worship fained gods.

And thus farre concerning open enemies: now concerning dissembled enemies.

The dissembled enemies of Christ and the true Church, are those who vnder the name of Christ do fight against him, and by many lying signes seduce men.

And they are eyther Antichristes, or false Christs.

Antichrists are the dissembled enemies of Christ, who euery manner of way are against the doctrine of Christ, whose followers they professe themselues to be. 1. Iohn. 2.18.22. & 4.3. & 2. Ioh. vers. 7.

And the same are also called false Prophets. Matth. 7.15.

Antichrist is two fold: for either he is against one part or other onely of the Christian doctrine, or else almost against the whole bodie of it.

Of the first kind are all Heretikes.

An Heretike is he who doth erre in the foundation of eternall saluation, that is to say, who doth fight against eyther the perfon or office of Christ, and doth stubbornely perseuere in errour.

Many such haue been euen from the times of the Apostles, and yet also there are some, as Cerinthus, Valentinus, Marcion, Sabellius, Arrius, Nestorius, Ertiches, Pelagius, and others.

Of the latter kind is that notorious aduersary of Christ, who by an excellency & principally is called Antichrist. 2. Thess. 2.7. and that false Prophet. Reuel. 16.13.

In this place especially two things are to be considered: first Antichrist himselfe: secondly the Church of Antichrist.

Concerning Antichrist himselfe, the question is both what he is, & who he should be.

That Antichrist is a man exercising a kingdome, the head of the vniuersall Apostacy, or falling away from the fayth, and professing the name of a Christian indeede, but yet setting himselfe both against Christ and the doctrine of Christ: hauing a double and supreme power, to wit, a spirituall and secular, boasting himselfe with deceaueable signes and miracles, an inchaunter making a compact with the deuill: an idolatrer, an hypocrite, a blasphemer, ambitious and proude, lawlesse, leading a single life, and forbidding marriage, and yet hee himselfe a filthy fornicatour and adulterer, a Sodomite, and that whoore of Babylon: abstayning from certaine kindes of meates, and yet giuen to riotousnesse: couetous, cousening men of their money, wily, giuen to vanitie, alyer, cruell, a tyrant, a persecuter & murtherer of the Saints, vaunting himselfe as God, and lifting vp himselfe against all powers and maiesties, both in earth and also in heauen, arrogating to himselfe the deuine power and absolute dominion of Christ, by a double and fourth fall that is to say, by the Romaine Monarchie out of the rubbishes thereof by litle and litle, rising and increasing by the power & forcible working of Sathan, in the citie compassed with seuen hils, that is to say, at Rome: and in the temple of God, that is to say, in the Church, but he shall be discouered in the last times of the world, and at the length by the glorious comming of Christ, shall vtterly be abolished. 2. Thess. 2.3. Dan. 7.8. Reuel. 17.1. & 18.3. & 13.11. and euery where throughout the Reuelations.

Thus farre is shewed what Antichrist is: now who it is.

THAT ANTICHRISR IS THAT POPI OF ROME: euen as both the Canon lawe, and also the liues and actes of the Bishoppes of Rome doe expressely shew.

Thus farre concerning Antichrist himselfe: now concerning the Church of Antichrist.

The Church of Antichrist, is the Church of Rome, falsely called Apostolicall and Catholike, wheras it is indeede an Apostaricall Church, that beast, and indeede disguising it selfe, and which doth represent the liuely image of the Monarchy of the Romaines, heretofore defaced of their gouernement, power, honour, and seat among all Nations Reuel. 11.7.8. and 13.3. and so forward, and euery where in the Reuelations: and experience also doth watnesse the same.

Of this Church there be two parts: to wit, the head, and the members.

The head of this Church of Antichrist, is Antichrist himselfe, the Pope of Rome, the sonne of perdition, and minister of the Dragon.

The members of it be eyther the Clergie, or the Lai·y.

The Clergy are those vncleane spirits comming out of the mouth of the Dragon, of that beast and false Prophet. Reuel. 16.13.

Of them there be three orders: Cardinals, false. Bishops and the filthy heape of Canonists, scholemen, and Monkes.

Cardinals are those vncleane spirits, comming forth of the mouth of the Dragon, of that beast and false Prophet, who goe to the Kings of the earth, and of the whole world, honored by that Antichrist of Rome with a

Cardinals hatte, and sent out that euen like frogs, by their clamorous and vnpleasant craking they might be importunate, which all men, to the intent they may gather them to the battle against God. Reuel. 16.13.14.

False Bishops are vncleane spirits, cōming out of the mouth of the Dragon of that same beast & false Prophet, who for a great price do buy their cope at Rome, and haue speciall iurisdiction, both ciuill and ecclesiasticall.

That heape of Canonists, Scholemen, and Monkes, are vncleane spirites comming out of the mouth of the Dragon, of that same beast and false Prophet, euery one according to his place vnderpropping the sea of Rome by murders and lyes.

But amongest the Monkes, those newe Monkes now adayes haue the cheifty, who by a false name are called Iesuits, whereas they are indeede Esauites or Iebusites.

So much concerning Antichrist: now concerning false Christs.

False Christs, are dissembled enemies of Christ, who vaunt themselues to be Christ. Matth. 24.26. Mar. 13.21. Luk. 17.23.

Such were Simon Magus, Bencocab, Dauid Gorgius, who was burnt at Basill.

The end of the first Booke of the partitions of diuintie.

THE SECOND BOOKE OF THE DEFINITIONS AND PARTITIONS OF DIUINITIE, FRAMED ACCORDING TO THE RULES OF A NATURALL METHODE, BY AMANDUS POLANUS OF POLANSDORFE.

Of good workes.

THE second part of the word of God, is concerning good workes, that is to say, which prescribeth and commandeth what works are to be done by the faithfull, that so men may performe thankefulnes due to God, for the deliuerance from sin and eternall death. Phil. 1.27. Iam. 2.20. Tit. 3.8.

Good workes are workes commanded by God, which are done of a true faith, to the glory of God alone. Rom. 14.13. Heb. 11.6.

And yet they are before God neither righteousnes it selfe nor any part of righteousnes, neither haue they any whit of merit in them. Esa. 64.6. Rom 3.28. Ephes 2.8.9. Luk. 17.10.

Euery singular good worke hath two sins set against it: the one as disagreeing, the other as contrarie.

The former of them is hypocrisie, that is to say, a fayning of godlinesse and honesty, or if you will, a new found godlinesse, the workes whereof doe seeme to haue some affinity and agreement with good workes: and therefore they doe oftentimes delude men with a shew and nearenesse of goodnesse: but in very deede are diuerse from them, eyther because they are not commaunded by God, but are fayned and cōmanded by men, vnder the opinion of vprightnes: or although they are commanded by God, yet they are done of hypocrisie either to deceiue others, or for the shewe of godlines, after the manner of the Pharises. Although sometime there may be more differēces or disagreemēts then one.

But the sinne which is opposed to a good work as contrary therto, is that which is simply contrary to it.

And euen as the summe of our faith is comprehended in the Creed of the Apostles, so the law of God is the direction and rule of good workes.

Both the adioints and also the kindes of good workes are to be considered.

The adioynts of good works are two fold: some if we respect God, and some if we respect men.

If we respect God they are two fold, that is, the childlike feare of God, and subiection that we owe to God.

The childlike feare of God, is a feare of the anger and iudgement of God against sin, whereby we are stirred vp reuerently to obey God and flie sinne. Or else the childlike feare of God, is that whereby we feare, as the chiefest euill of all, least we displease God through disobedience. Psal. 5.8. Such a feare is in the elect, and it consisteth in three things.

First, that we set before our eyes God always beholding all our workes.

Secondly, that we acknowledge and reuerence him as the witnesse and reuenger of all our thoughts, words, and workes.

Thirdly, that there be nothing which we feare more then to offende God, being so louing a father, and to stirre vp his anger and iudgement against vs.

Against this feare of God is opposed, both a causelesse feare, and the seruile or slauish feare of God, & also security or carelesnes: the two former as disperate or disagreeing, the other as contrary.

A causeles feare is to feare where no feare is. Psal. 14. This is an hypocriticall feare, as is that also of the Papists, who feare the wrath of God, when they breake foolish traditions, as when they will not eate flesh on daies forbidden by the Bishop of Rome, and doe not feare the anger of God, when they doe stiffely and stubburnly defend Idolatry, & do persecute godly men and innocentes with sword and fire.

The seruile feare of God, is the feare of Gods wrath, and deuine iudgement against sin, by which the vngodly are so smitten, that they flee from God, and chafe against him. And that is in the wicked, as in Cain, Saul, & Iudas Iscariot, of which feare mentiō is made, 1. Iohn. 4.18.

Securitie, is to liue without care and without the feare of Gods anger, and of his diuine iudgement against sin. Pro. 28.14. Matt. 12.44.

Securitie is two fold: either in the vngodly, or in the godly.

Securitie in the vngodly, or if you wil call it Epicureall & giant-like contempt of God, is an amazednes or benummednes altogether neglecting the wrath and iudgment of God.

Securitie in the godly, is a cold & languishing feare of God, thē especially appearing in them, when they be in prosperitie.

So much concerning the feare of God: now concerning subiection vnto God.

Subiection vnto God, is that by which we submit our selues to God, as to our Lord, to performe to him the obedience of the Law.

The obedience of the law, is a perfect conformitie of al thoughts, motions, and actions, inward and outward, to the law of God.

Hitherto concerning the adioynts of good workes as they respect God.

The adioynts of good workes in respect of men are two fold: either as concerning our selues, or our neighbour.

In respect of our selues there are required chearefulnes, conscience, cōstancy, & wisdom.

Chearefulnesse is that, by which any man of his owne accord freely and willingly doth with ioy obey the lawe of God. Psal. 40.9. & 110.3. Col. 3.23.

To it is opposed rashnes & cōpulsion: the former as disagreeing, the other as contrary.

Rashnes is an inconsiderate forwardnes or wilfulnes of doing something, vnder the pretext of obeying God, whē as yet a man knoweth not whether that which he doth or will doe, be commanded by God. And of this sort is that rage that is in Idolaters, who are ready to exercise & cōmit Idolatry, and to do euery thing cōmanded by their sacrificing Priests.

Compulsion is that, wherby a mā being cōpelled, doth obey either for feare of punishmēt, or for shame before others: therfore also such an obedience is displeasing vnto God.

Conscience is that sparke of right reason, which remaineth in mā as yet vndefaced, & is that bewrayer & iudge of good & euil deeds. It is a bridle before sin, sometime to stay the rage of it, and a scourage after sin committed, to afflict the heart or mind.

Constancy is a perpetuall will and study to obey Gods law, or else it is a stable and perpetual abiding in the obedience of Gods law. Eph. 4.14.15. Dan. 1.8.

Or else, Constancy is a perpetuall will to do good workes.

To this there is opposed stubburnnes & inconstancy: the one as disparat or disagreeing, the other as contrary.

Stubburnnes is an abiding or perseuering in euill, as in vngodly opinions, superstitions and wickednes contrary to conscience.

Inconstancy is a rash changing of the mind or will from good to euill. 2. Chron. 24.21. Ierem. 26.8.16.

Wisedome, is that by which wee obserue comelinesse in euery action. Eph. 5.15.16.17. that is to say, by which we obserue what we are to doe, how, in what place, at what time, before whom, that all things may be done in a conuenient place, time, and manner.

Of wisdom there are two parts, a perceiuing or foresight, & vprightnesse of choice.

A perceiuing or foresight, is a carefull and diligent considering, what is comely in euery action. It is otherwise called circumspection.

The vprightnes of choise, is that by which we doe will & choose that which we perceiue to be meete. Psal. 119.173.

Therefore by wisedome, counsels and deliberations are directed in the choise of honest and profitable things, and al actions so caried, that conueniencie of place, time, and persons, and of other circumstances is obserued.

So Paul willeth that our seruing of God be according to reason. Rom. 12.1. So the same Paul doth commaund vs to obserue oportunitie in the exercise of vertues. Rom. 13.11.

Singular wisdome is required in the choise of euill things.

Of two euils the lesse euill is to be chosen. But this rule is to be vnderstood of the euill of the punishment which is contrary to profitable goodnesse, and not of the euill of the offence, contrary to honest goodnesse. For if God forbid both euils, neither of them is to be done.

Therefore in euils of offence or sinne there must be no choise: that is to say▪ the euils of offence & sin it selfe, must at no hand be chosen, but all euils are to be shunned a like.

In euils of punishmēt there may be choise, as if one being taken in warre, or falling into the hands of a theefe, might chuse whether he will redeeme himselfe with money, or whether he will loose his life: it is better to loose his money, then his life.

So 2. Sam. 24 12. To Dauid, when hee had sinned by numbring the people, the Lord offereth a choise of three fold punishment, of which he should chuse one which he would, namely, either seuen yeares famine through the whole kingdome, or warre in which hee should flee three moneths before his enemies pursuing him, or three daies pestilence Consider now (saith the Prophet Gad) and looke what I shall answere to him that sent mee. Therefore saith Dauid to God: I am distressed aboue measure: but it is better to fall into the hand of the Lord (because his mercies are many) then into the hands of men.

Of the euils wherof (euen for the profession of true religiō) choise is offered to one that is altogether innocent, no choise ought to bee made: but we must wait what God wil, & patiently beare what soeuer the tyrant hath decreed: least if thou chuse willingly punishmēt & death, thou wrap thy selfe in suspition of hauing committed some wickednes, & dost giue occasiō to spread slanders of thy fame to the posterity; for otherwise thou wouldst not willingly haue chosen punishment, if thou hadst not binguiltie to thyself of some fault. There is an exāple of such a spiritual wisdom in the french history, in the prince of Condie himselfe. Charles IX. sent for the Condie to come to him, & propoūded to him three cōditions, of which he shold chuse one: namely to goe to Masse, or to death, or to perpetuall imprisonmēt. The Cōdie answered him, that he would (God so assisting him) neuer so trespasse as to chuse the first. Of the other two he left the one or the other of them to the will & pleasure of the King, & yet doubted not, but God would gouerne all that action by his prouidence.

To wisdome there is opposed wylinesse, or deceipt, and rashnesse: the former as disparate or disagreeing, the other as contrary.

Wylines is an obseruation of our own profite in some thing, and that with the hurt of another. For wisedome is in good things: but wilinesse in euill things.

Rashnesse is a wilfulnesse or violence to do any thing without coūsel & reason. Pro. 15.22.

Spirituall wisedome, is specially seene in beating backe and ouercomming the temptations of Sathan.

Hitherto we haue spoken of the adioynts of good workes as in respect of our selues: now concerning the adioynts of good workes, in respect of our neighbour.

The adioints of good works in respect of our neighbour, are zeale for the glory of God, and care to shunne offences.

Zeale for the glory of God, is a vehement greife of mind, and indignation against the things which are done contrary to Gods law, with an indeuour to hinder those sins in time and place conuenient. Iohn. 2.14. Psal. 68.10. 1. King. 19.10. Act. 17.16. Num. 25.11. 2. Cor. 7.7. & 11. 2. Psal. 119.139.

This zeale ought to be ioyned with knowledge, that is, with a sound knowledge & spiritual wisdome of Gods wil, and of the truth.

To it is opposed zeale without knowledge and benummednesse.

Zeale without knowledge is a blind wilfulnes & violence, or an incōsiderate indignatiō against those things which are either right & good, or if they be done contrary to the lawe of God, they are done of ignorāce or infirmity. Ro. 10.2. Phil. 3.6. Act. 21.20. & 22.3. Gal. 1.14.

And it doth arise either of the ignorance of the truth, or of the charity and edification of our neighbour neglected.

Benummednesse is when any as it were a block is not touched at all, although he doth manifestly see many things to be done frowardly and stubburnely against God.

Care to auoid offences, is when whatsoeuer we doe, we haue alwaies a respect that we be not an offence to others, but that by our example we may rather edifie them.

So much concerning the adioynts of good workes: their kinds follow.

Good works are two fold: that is either the workes of Gods worship, or of vertue. The former, that is, Gods worship, is commanded in the first table of the ten commandements: the other in the second.

The worship of God is an honor to be giuen to God alone according to his commandemēt; If I be your father, where is my honor? I will not giue my glory to an other: that he that honoureth the sonne, might honour the father also: that they may glorifie your father in heauē. Pro. 3.9. Honor God with thy riches.

Atheisme, witchcraft, Idolatry, and superstition are contrary to the true and sincere worship of God.

Atheism is whē some beastly natures of mē, do deny that there is any God: or at the least that there is any prouidence of God. Psal. 14.

Witchcraft is a couenāting with the deuils ye enemies of God, that by their help things not necessary may be knowen and effected either for the fulfilling of euill lusts, or for ostentatiō▪ or to the cōmodity of life, or else that they might receiue by them those things which are to be asked and looked for from God alone. Deut. 18.11.

Idolatry is a sinne, when the worship that is due to God alone, is translated to the creatures. Gen. 31.30.34. Exod. 12.12. Iere. 43.13. Exod. 32.1.2. &c. Iud. 17.3.4.

The worshipping of bread, or of the God Maozim in the Papisticall masse, and as also the worship of Images, are speciall kinds of Idolatry.

Superstition, is a sinne, when the effects of Gods fauour, or some naturall force, is attributed to a thing or gesture without Gods commaundement, or without natural causes. Col. 2.23. Gen. 32.32. Iud. 18.27. 1. Sam. 5.5. Act. 17.22.

There are infinit kinds of this superstition amongst the Papists: among which the exorcisme, or as we may call it coniuration of creatures is notorious.

Exorcisme is a superstition, through which the sacrificing priest adiureth the euill spirit by heauenly things, and doth boldly enough, and by his authority, command him, that he depart out of the infant that is to be baptized.

The worship of God, is either onely inward, or else both inward and outward. Deu. 6.5. & 10 12. Mat. 1.8.

The onely inward worship of God, is that which doth consist in the affectiō of the mind onely. Deut. 6.5.

And that is the true knowledge of God, loue towards God, humility, confidence in God, and patience.

The true knowledge of God, is the inward worship of God, when we know God so, as he hath manifested himselfe in his word.

To it is contrary the ignorance of God, which is not to know those things concerning God, which euery one ought to know. Furthermore false opinions touching God, are contrary to it.

Loue towards God, is the inward worship of God, when we do loue God so earnestly, that we do all his commaundements with a certaine ioyfulnesse. 1. Ioh. 5.3. 1. Tim. 1. Deut. 6. Mat. 22.

To it is contrary the hatred of God, which is by reason of the turning away of our nature from God, and from the iustice of God, and through inclination to sinne, to flee from God, and to be angry with him, accusing and punishing sinne. Rom. 8.7.

To it also is contrary, an inordinate loue of himself or of any of the creatures, which is to preferre a mans owne lusts, will, life, or glory, before Gods will and glory, and wickedly to neglect, and offend him rather then to forgoe those things we loue. Mat. 10.37.

Humility is the inward worship of God, when we acknowledgeing our owne misery, cast away all confidence in our own strength, and do acknowledge that all good thinges which are in vs, and which are done by vs, do not proceede of any worthinesse or ability of our owne, but of the free goodnesse of God. 1. Cor. 4.7. Iob. 1.21.

Poore in spirite that is to say, humble, may he be said to be, who doth acknowledge that he hath no good thing of his owne nature, or by himselfe, but rather that he is naked and poore, and voide of all good things, and receiueth all such things freely from God.

To it is opposed, a fained humility and pride.

Fained humility belongeth to hypocrites. Col. 2.23. as of the Pharisies. Mat. 6.6. Of the Anabaptists and Muncks, who will be humble without lowlinesse, poore without want, rich without labour, as Bernard saith.

Pride is a sinne, when any one without the knowledge of his own infirmity, doth loue, extoll, and magnifie himselfe for some giftes he hath, and doth swell and trust in his owne wisedome, holinesse and strength, and attributeth to himselfe more then is in him, & despiseth others. Prou. 8.13. & 16.5. Reuel. 3.17.

Thus farre concerning humility: now concerning confidence in God.

Confidence in God, is the inward worship of God, when all humaine confidence either in our selues, or in other creatures, being layed aside, we do rest in God alone. Ier. 17.5. and so forward.

To it is opposed tempting of God, confidence in creatures, and distrust.

Tempting of God, is presumption, and confidēce, imagining vnder a foolish pretext of confidence in God, that we shall effect and performe some things without the word & reuealed will of God: as if any will not vse meanes ordayned by God: to such a sinne the Deuill tempted Christ. Mat• 4.6.7.

Confidence in creatures, is a sinne, when any doth put his trust in riches, or in the fauour of Princes, and of other men. Eph. 5.5. Mat 6.24. Psal. 146.3. Iere. 17.5. & 48.

Distrust is a sinne, when any doth not rest in God, nor stay vppon his helpe alone, but giueth place to fearefulnesse, trembling and anguish, and doth seeke meanes and helpes forbidden and not graunted. 1. Sam. 28.5.6.7.8.

Confidence in God, is either a liuely faith, or hope in God.

A liuely faith, is not onely a knowledge and consent, whereby a man beleeueth that whatsoeuer the word of God hath commanded to be beleeued, is true, but also a firme & constant confidence, by which euery one doth for himselfe obtaine and get the benefits promised by God.

Or else, a iustifying faith, is a confidence whereby euery one certainely beleeueth for himselfe, that the merite of Christ is assuredly imputed and giuen to him.

Faith doth receiue not only spirituall but euen bodily benefites also. Mat. 9.22. Christ sayth to the womā that had an issue of bloud; Thy faith hath saued thee.

Therefore a liuely faith is either of spirituall or bodily good things.

The proper duties thereof are two.

The first, that by it euery one is certainely perswaded for himselfe, that the promises of God do also pertaine to himselfe.

The other, that by that alone as by the only hand• we receiue and lay hold on the benefites offered by God.

Therefore also by that alone we are iustified before God.

To be iustified by faith onely in Iesus Christ, is by faith alone as by a hand and only instrument to take hold of, and to apply to himselfe the righteousnesse of Christ, purchased by the obedience of his death.

To a sauing faith is opposed incredulity, doubting infolden or hidden faith, and temporary faith.

Incredulity is that, which when a man hath heard and known Gods word, doth not consent to the same, and specially to the promise of Grace.

Doubting is neither fi mely to consent to the word of God, & in that word to the promise of Grace especially, neither altogether to resist the same, but to flow: now into one part, and anone faintly to incline to the other part.

An infolden or hidden faith is to submit his sense obediently to the Church, and to beleeue things not vnderstood, and to embrace for trueth, whatsoeuer the Church hath prescribed, and to post ouer to the Church the labour of enquiring and knowing the same, & not to be carefull whether the Church prescribe true things or not.

This deuise of an infolden or hidden faith was inuented by schoolemen, and after them the Vbiquitaries haue diuersly commended it, vnder which name, decking a most grosse ignoraunce, they go about to delude the sillie common people to their great destruction.

Temporarie faith, is to embrace the truth for a time, but without regeneration and confidence of the promise of the grace of God, and therefore in time of temptations and persecutions, to be ouercome through hope of profit and honor, and to cast away againe the profession of the trueth. Mat. 13.5.20.21. Luk 8.13. Act. 8.13. Heb. 6.4.

So much concerning faith: now concerning hope in God.

Hope in God is confidence in God, by which we vndoubtedly looke for the benefites of God to come, but especially eternall life to be giuen freely for Christ his sake, and the mitigating of the present crosse, or deliuerāce from it, according to Gods counsell. 1. Pet. 1.13.

Faith doth receiue the present benefites of God, but hope doth looke for those which are to come.

To hope is opposed the hope of Papists, doubting concerning the receiuīng of Gods benefites, and desperation.

Papisticall hope is a sinne, when any for the Buls and pardons of that damnable Romaine Antichrist and his indulgences, or else for some good worke of his owne, especially not commaunded by God, as peregrinations to the sepulchres of Saincts, buildings of Monasteries, giftes to Churches, or for taking a Munckes Cowle, and so for that doth falsely perswade himselfe that he shall obtaine eternall life.

Doubting concerning the receiuing of Gods benefits is a sinne, whē any doth doubt of eternall life, and defence, and deliuerance in temptation.

Desperation, is to esteeme and iudge his owne sinnes greater then the merite of the Sonne of God: and to refuse the mercy of God offered in the Sonne of God, the mediatour of God and man: and therefore not to looke for the benefites promised by God to the beleeuers, but to be vexed with the horrible feeling of Gods wrath, & with feare of subsequent casting away into eternall punishment, and to abhor and hate God as cruell and a tyrant. Gen. 4.13. 1. Thess. 4.13.

So much concerning confidence: now concerning patience.

Patience is the inward worship of God, when we submit our selues to God, quietly to beare the crosse layed vpon vs by him. Num. 16.46. Iob. 1.20. & 2.10.

To it is opposed an hypocriticall tollerating or bearing, and impatiency.

An hypocriticall tollerating or bearing, is a suffering of torments, brought vppon them by their owne accord: as in Heremites, in Munckes: in whippers, who do beat themselues with rods.

Impatiency is a sinne, when a man will not obey God in bearing the griefes which God hath layd vpon him, but is angry and murmureth against God, & chiefly against them that hurt him, as the Isaelites. Exod. 5.21. & 14.11. &. 16.3. & 17.2.3.

<u>Hitherto concerning that worship of God which is only inward: now concerning that which is both inward and outward.</u>

The worship of God both inward & outward, is that which comprehend the obedience of the soule and body. Deut. 5.19. & 6.5. & 10.12. Rom. 12.1.

And it hath two obiects, that is, calling vpon God and thankesgiuing· and also the confession of the trueth, and the obseruing of the Ecclesiasticall rites or orders.

Calling vpon God is the worship of God, by which we do religiously call vppon God. Psal. 50.18. & 116.13.

To it is opposed an idolatrous inuocation, and the omitting of inuocation, or sinne.

An idolatrous inuocation is a sinne, when that is called vpon which is not God.

And of this first, is the inuocation or sinne of the Gentiles, Turkes, Iewes, and Papists.

The omitting of inuocation is a sin, when inuocation so straightly commaunded by God is omitted, as though God had no need of it.

Calling vppon God is either prayer or an oath.

Prayer is a calling vppon God, by which we aske of God such good things as are necessary for the soule and body, and contrariwise do pray, that euill things may be remoued Gen. 17.18. & 24.12. & 28. 2. & ·2.11. Exod. 8.12. 1. Sam. 17.19. 1. King. 8.15.

And that ⟨◊⟩ either the absolute seruice of the deity, or prayer proper to the mediator.

The absolute seruice of the deity, is that which is properly directed to the deity: and with that also wee worshippe Christ as hee is God, and by which we attribute vnto him the honour of omnipotency, knowing all things, and being euery where present.

Prayer proper to the mediator, is that worship which is giuen to Christ, both in respect of his person and of his office, as to that mediator that is God and man.

For as the acknowledgement of Christ consisteth in the acknowledgement of his person and office: so in inuocation we must thinke of Christ, after either manner.

First, he is to be called vppon as God, the giuer of good things, with the Father and the holy Spirite.

Secondly, we must thinke of him as of a mediatour, and intercessour, for whose sake we beleeue that wee are receiued and heard.

That worship of the mediatour is one, not in respect or degree, but in number.

And as our faith in the acknowledgment of Christ, doth put a difference betweene the natures: so also in the worshipping of him.

Therefore he the mediatour is worshipped, not for his humanities sake, which is created, but because of his eternall and omnipotent deity. For the deity the Creator of all things, is the proper subiect of religious worship: and not the humanity, because it is a creature. Cyrillus writing to Theodosius the king concerning the right faith, saith; Shall we therefore worship Emmanuell, that is God with vs, as a man? Be it farre from vs: for this sinne were a dotage, deceipt and errour. For in this wee should not differ from those, who do worship the creature more then the creator and maker.

And as faith doth attribute to him according to either nature, that which it ought according to the Scriptures: so it doth demaund that in the worke of hearing, as in the perfection of his duetie and obedience, he should worke according to either nature that which is his owne to do.

According to the deity, that he might behold the hearts, heare the sighes of his seruants, giue the holy Spirite, and other good things according to his vnmeasurable wisdome and power.

But according to the humanity, that he might of his own humaine will approoue the prayers and hearings of his people, and in that might do that which is proper to him. So the Church prayeth. Reuel. 22.20. Euen come thou Lord Iesus: in which prayer it doth aske, not that made manifest in his God-head, he might come in the clouds, but manifested in his humanity: and so one and that selfe same Lord Iesus might deliuer and glorifie the Church by his diuine omnipotency or almighty power.

Thus much concerning the distribution of prayer: now concerning the forme of prayer.

Of all other, the Lords prayer is the best forme of prayer.

The Lords prayer, is that which our Lord Christ himselfe hath taught vs. Mat. 6.9. Luke 11.20. Our Father which art in heauen, and so forth.

Of the Lords prayer are foure parts: an entrance, petitions, a confirmation, and a conclusion.

Of the entrance there are two parts: the first teacheth vs whom we ought to call vppon: namely our father.

Our father is God.

Now we call God father, for two causes.
- 1 Because he hath begot the sonne to himselfe from eternity, to wit, Iesus Christ.
- 2 Because he hath adopted vs to be his sonnes, for Christ his sake.

But in our prayers we call him father, for three causes.
- 1 That we being about to pray might find a distinction between our inuocation and the prayers of Infidels, turning our selues to this God, who hath manifested himselfe in his sonne Iesus Christ.
- 2 That a child-like feare and reuerence of God might be stirred vp in vs.
- 3 That we might pray with confidence, certainly assuring our selues that we are heard of God, as of a mercifull father, because he hath adopted vs to be his sonnes, because we are members of Christ, because we call vpon him by Christ.

But we call him our Father for two causes.
- 1 That so we might thinke, that we are to pray not only for our selues, but for other men also, especially for those who are members with vs in the body of Christ, & sonnes of the same father in heauen.
- 2 That we may pray the more boldly, thinking this, that the whole Church, and euen the mediator, as our brother, doth pray with vs.

This is the first part of the entrance: the second followeth.

The second part is this: which art in Heauen.

That God is in heauen, it meaneth, that he onely is omnipotent, and alone can giue vs those things which we aske of him.

God truely is euery where. Iere. 23.23.24. Esa. 66.1. But heauen is as it were the ordinary Pallace of God, in which is his throne, and the chiefest glory of God doth appeare: because God doth most magnifically manifest himself in heauen to the Angels & blessed soules. Psal. 115.16. Psal. 19.

But these words, which art in heauen, are added for fiue causes.
- 1 That we might not imagine any earthly and carnall matter of the heauenly maiesty of God.

- 2 That we being about to pray, might lift vp our minds from the earth to heauen, Psal. 25. & 121.
- 3 That we might expect from the omnipotency and almighty power of God, what things soeuer are necessary for soule & body.
- 4 That we might be mindfull of this, that our God hath all gouernment of heauen and earth, that he is present euery where, and that he heareth and helpeth those that cal on him.
- 5 That we should not direct or tie the worship of God to any place or thing besides his commandement.

So much concerning the entrance of the Lords prayer: the petitions follow.

The petitions of the Lordes prayer are two fold: the three former pertaine to the glorie of God, and the three later to our own necessitie.

The first petition is this:Hallowed be thy name.

In it wee aske the hallowing of Gods name.

The hallowing of Gods name is the glorifying of God.

And that is done both by true faith, and also by good works.

Therefore the sense and meaning of the first petition is this; Grant that we may glorifie thee by true faith and good works.

We sanctifie Gods name by true faith, when we rightly acknowledge God and his workes.

We sanctifie Gods name by good works, both when we worship God aright, and also when we desire and labour for vertue and well doing, and that to this end, that the most holy name of God might not be slaundered through our meanes, but rather that other seeing our good workes, might glorifie our heauenly Father.

The second petition is this:Let thy kingdome come,

In it we aske the comming of the kingdome of God.

The comming of the kingdome of God, is the gouerning of the Church.

And this comming of Gods kingdome is two fold: either to the whole Church, or to the seuerall members of it.

The cōming of gods kingdome to the whole Church, is when God defendeth the Church.

And that two waies: both in preseruing & encreasing his owne church, & in destroying the church of the deuill, or sathās synagogue.

The comming of Gods kingdome to euery mēber of the church, is when God doth so by his word and spirite gouerne euery one, that he doth subiect them more and more to himselfe and the obedience of his will.

The sense therefore of the second petition is this; Gouerne thy Church, and the seuerall members of the Church by thy spirit and word.

The third petition is this:Thy will bee done, as in heauen, so in earth also.

In it we aske that all of vs might obey Gods will, and that all wicked lustes being tamed, we might wholly and altogether serue God, and that so readily and willingly as the holy Angels in heauen do.

Will doth here signifie that which is acceptable to God, and that also which he therfore requireth of vs.

<u>The three former petitions haue been thus expounded: the three later follow.</u>

The three later petitions pertaine to our necessity, and that both as in respect of the body, as the fourth petition: and also as in respect of the soule, as the fift and sixt.

The fourth petition is this:Giue vs this day our daily bread.

In it we aske the sustentation and nourishment of this temporall life.

Daily bread, is whatsoeuer is necessarie for the vpholding and preseruation of this present life.

God indeed hath commaunded vs to get it with the labour of our hands, but yet we aske it of God, because neither our labour, neither those thing which are gotten by our labour, do or can profite vs without Gods blessing, which it selfe also is part of dayly bread.

But if thou art rich and abounding, yet as if thou were needy, pray daily for the blessed vse of thy riches, thinke that full sellers, and full store-houses, or chests, may be sodenly emptyed, except they be kept by the Lords hand: yea except the Lord shall season with his blessing the meat and drinke that we take in, they that eat shall sterue for hunger, & they that drinke shall waxe dry with thirst. Eze. 4.14. Ye shall eat and not be satisfied. Leuit. 26.26.

Now we name it our bread indeede, and yet we aske that God would giue it vs, because that by the gift of God it is become ours: neither can any thing be ours, or become ours except God giue it.

We name it our bread, that so being content with that, we might not desire another mans.

And we call it our bread and not mine, that so euery one might know, that he ought to aske bread necessary not for himself alone, but for his neighbour also.

Lastly, we aske dayly bread, and pray that the same may be dayly giuen vs, for foure causes.

- 1 That a distrustfull carefulnesse for to morow might be taken out of our minds.

- 2 That we might remember, that for daily bread we haue neede of daily prayers.
- 3 That we might be daily admonished of the shortnes of this our bodily life, as though we should liue to day onely.
- 4 That we might not immoderately & greedily desire or couet any thing besides that which God hath prescribed.

The fift petition is this:And forgiue vs our trespasses, as we forgiue those that trespasse against vs.

In it we aske the forgiuenesse of sinnes, or iustification.

And when God in his eternall couenant had willingly & freely promised vs forgiuenesse of sinnes, he hath also bound vs to himselfe by the answering againe of a good conscience to forgiue our brethren.

So that he is not bound to keepe his promise with vs, except we also continue in the obligation, couenant, or condition to be performed on our part.

Our forgiuing therefore is not a cause of Gods forgiuing: for God first hath freely promised vs forgiuenesse, when as yet wee were his enemies: and besides he hath bound vs to himselfe to pardon our brethren also.

The cause can not be after his proper effect.

But our forgiuing of them is after Gods forgiuing of vs.

Therefore our forgiuing is not the cause of Gods forgiuing.

The assumption is certaine, for they only can pardon their bretheren, to whom God hath forgiuen their sinnes: and by this testimonie we feele in our harts that our sinnes are pardoned vs, if wee be fully purposed with our selues from our hearts to pardon all those who haue offended vs.

The sixt petition is this:And leade vs not into temptation, but deliuer vs from euill.

In it we aske both that we our selues may be gouerned by the holy spirite and word, least we should fall into sinne. And this gouerning is part of our regeneration or sanctification, and also deliuerance from euils, that is to say, from the snares of Sathan, from the deceipts of the world, and from the entisements of the flesh, as causes of sinne.

Thus hath the second part of the Lordes prayer bene handled: the third followeth.

The third part of the Lords prayer is a cōfirmation, which conteyneth three argumēts, by which our faith is confirmed, that God doth certainly heare our prayers. Two arguments are drawen from the adioynts of God, the third from the end of hearing.

The first adioynt of God is this: because he is king hauing rule ouer all things.

The second, because he is able, who can giue vs all things which we aske.

The argument from the ende is, that he might be praysed and glorified for euer, because he is God, and a most bountifull and mercifull father.

Hitherto we haue handled the third part of the Lords prayer: the conclusion remaineth.

The conclusion of the Lords prayer consisteth in one word. Amen, which is both a wish that those things may be ratified, which we aske, and also a note of confidence, wherby we shew that we are perswaded, that God hath certainly heard our prayers.

Blessing is a peculiar kinde of prayer, and that is, whereby we aske good things for other men at the hands of God.

And that is due to all, whether friends or enemies.

To it is opposed execration or cursing.

Against praier to God is opposed, wicked prayer, idolatrous prayer, the omitting of prayers, a vaine babling, and tediousnesse in praying.

A wicked prayer, is an asking of those things at Gods hande which are contrary to Gods will and law.

An idolatrous prayer, is that which is directed and made either to the fayned gods of the Gentiles, or to dead Saints: and of this sort are the prayers of Ethnickes and Papists.

The omitting of prayers, is a sin when any doth omit praiers, as though he did not want the helpe and blessing of God.

A vaine babling is the reciting of long or many prayers, with the vaine noyse of the lips without the true motion of the hart, & without faith: hither pertaine the bellowing of the Monkes in the Churches.

Tediousnesse in praier is a sinne when any one hauing a desire of other things, maketh prayer with a wandring mind, and a hart that desireth the prayers were ended.

Hitherto concerning prayer: now concerning an oath.

An oath is a calling vpon God, by which we call him (as the onely searcher of the hart and raynes) for a witnesse of our speech, that so he may giue testimony to the truth, and aueng and punish the deceipt, if we wittingly deceiue others thereby. Deut. 6.13. and 10.20. Rom. 1.9. 2. Cor. 1.23. & 11.31. Phil. 1.8.

The parts of an oath are two: that is, taking God to witnesse, and cursing.

Taking God to witnesse, is that by which the swearer doth cite God as a witnesse of his asseueration. Rom. 1.9. Deut. 6.13. & 10.29. Ios. 23.7. Esa. 65.16. Ier. 5.7. & 12.16.

Cursing is that by which the swearer doth vow and tie himselfe to the punishment of periury, that he may be accursed before God, and God may punish him, if he wittingly deceiue. 1. King. 2.23.

An oath is two fold: to wit, offered, or a voluntary oath of a mans owne accord.

An offered oath, is that which is offered by the Magistrate or Iudge, or the aduerse party: in Greeke it is called swearing. Heb. 6.16.

A voluntary oath, or oath of a mans owne accord, but yet taken, a mans calling forcing him thereunto, is that which is done that we might defend either our owne or other mens good name & life: as Paul by calling God to witnesse, affirmeth that he spake the truth. Rom. 9.1.

The refusing of a lawful oath, and a wicked oath, are contrary to the religion of an oath.

The refusing of a lawfull oath is a sin, whē any doth refuse to take an oath which either the Magistrate doth iustly require, or otherwise necessitie demandeth, vnder this condition, that faith may bee confirmed, and the truth established: that so both the glory of God may be set forth, and other mens safetie prouided for.

A wicked oath is a sinne, when a man doth sweare against the law of God.

And it is either a rash oath, or an Idolatrous oath, or els periury, or of an vnlawfull thing.

A rash oath is when any sweareth rashly, & without cause, of a certaine lightnes, and prophane custome: as if any being angry, sweareth that he will slay another.

An Idolatrous oath, is when a man sweareth by Saints, or other creatures.

Periurie is a sinne, when any wittingly and willingly deceiueth by an oath, whether it be in giuing testimonie, or in professing some thing of himselfe, or in the promise of his owne will. Exod. 20.7. Leuit. 19.12. Matth. 5.33. Iam. 5.12.

An oath of an vnlawfull thing is when any sweareth that he will doe that which is contrary to Gods word. Such was that of Iephte and of Herod.

So much concerning calling vpon God: now concerning thankesgiuing.

Thanksgiuing is the worship of God, whē we render due praise to God for good things giuen or promised Psal. 50.15.

The parts of it are two: the approbation of Gods workes and praysing of God.

The approbation of Gods workes, is a part of thankesgiuing, when wee allow all things whatsoeuer God doth because they are good, and therefore we do suffer them to please and like vs. So it becommeth vs also to allow of the iudgements of God, his prouidence and gouerning of tempests, of calmenesse, of rayne, of wars, of our health, of our household affayres and all other things. Mar. 7.37. Psal. 119.71.

The praysing of God is a part of thankesgiuing, when we prayse God in al his workes.

To it is adioyned the admiration of Gods workes, and the right estimation of them.

The admiration of Gods workes, is a part of the praysing God, when wee maruaile at his works, with the true motion of our hart. Psal. 8.2. Mar. 7.37. Matth. 9.33.

The right estimation of Gods workes, is a part of the praysing God, when we magnifie and extoll his workes. Psal. 8.2. and so forward, and 104 throughout.

To thankesgiuing is opposed an hypocriticall thankfulnesse, as is that of the Pharisie. Luk. 18.11. and ingratitude towardes God, which is a sinne when wee doe not acknowledge that we haue receiued of God whatsoeuer good thing we haue. Also whē one vseth Gods graces and giftes without thankesgiuing. Also when any findeth fault with the workes and iudgementes of God: or when any doth little esteeme the workes of God, and his iudgements: or when any is not content with that which God giueth him, and prescribeth God, what and how he ought to doe.

And thus farre concerning thankesgiuing: now concerning the confession of the truth.

The confession of the truth is the worship of God, when we do openly without feare professe the heauenly truth, as it is made knowen vnto vs out of the holy scripture. Matth. 10.32. 1. Pet. 3.15.

And that is done either with the mouth, or by martyrdome.

With the mouth, when we doe without doubtfulnesse and darkenesse professe that which we thinke with our heart. Rom. 10.10.

By martyrdome, when we giue testimony to the truth, by the crosse: yea when God shal see it so good, by death it selfe. 1. Pet. 2.20. & 3.14. & 4.12. Phil. 1.29.

To the confession of the truth, is opposed heresie, the corrupting of doctrine, blasphemy, and omitting of doctrine, the shunning of doctrine, the tediousnesse of doctrine, an vnseasonable confession, the dissembling of truth, and denying of truth.

Heresie is a sinne, when any erreth in the foundation of saluation, and stiffely or stubburnly perseuerteth in his error.

Therefore that wicked stubburnnesse of franticke men in the punishmēts which they suffer, either for sedition, as for example, of the Anabaptists, or for errors which are opēly blasphemous, as of Seruetus, who was burnt at Geneua in the yeare 1552. is not the confession of truth.

For these are not the martyrs of Christ, because the cause maketh a martyr not the martyrdome, as Cyprian saith, and Apollinaris; Where the truth of Christ is not, there is not the truth of martyrdome.

The corrupting of doctrine, is when men spread abroad any false thing of God or of his will.

Blasphemy is to speake of God, thing cōtrary to his nature and will. Leu. 24.

The omitting of doctrine, is a neglect of occasions & ability to teach others, & to bring them to the knowledge of the truth, especially our children or others, who are committed to our faithfulnesse and care.

The shunning of doctrine, is a sinne, when any doth shun conferences and speeches concerning God and heauenly things.

Tediousnes of doctrine is a sin, when any is cloyed, as we say, with the fulnesse of the word of God.

An vnseasonable confession, is that which is made without the necessity of a mans calling, or of doing some duty: and therfore neither the glory of God is set foorth by such a confession, neither the saluatiō of any is promoted, but rather eyther the scorning or obloquie of the truth, or the fiercenesse of the enemies is stirred thereby, specially against the godly.

The dissembling of the truth, is a sin, when any dissembleth the truth, where the glory of God, and safety of his neighbour requireth a true and full confession.

The denying of the truth is a sin, whē any doth deny the truth after he hath certainely knowen it.

The denying of the truth is two fold: either proceeding of infirmity, or willing.

The former is when any being vpon the suddaine, and with present and vnlooked for feare, ouercome and compelled, doth with his mouth indeede deny the truth, and that to shun some danger, but neuerthelesse keepeth it in his heart, neither falleth from it. Such a denying was that of Peter the Apostle who denyed Christ. Mat. 26.69. &c.

A willing denying of the truth is a sin, whē any denyeth the truth certainly knowen, being ouercome and compelled with no suddaine &

vnlooked for feare, but willingly & of purpose, eyther to keepe dignity, or life, or for hope to obtaine substance and riches.

And that is properly called Apostasie, that is to say, a wicked falling away frō the truth, as was that of Iulian the Apostata, and Francis Spira.

Hitherto concerning the confession of the truth: now concerning the obseruing of the Ecclesiasticall rites or ceremonies.

An Ecclesiasticall rite or ceremony is the worship of God, in which we worship God by outward meanes.

And it is eyther common to the olde and new Testament, or proper to eyther of them.

A rite common to the old and new Testament, is both the sanctifying of an holy day, and also a godly fast and vow.

The sanctifying or celebrating of an holy day, is an ecclesiasticall rite, when we resting from humaine and bodily labours, doe come together into the publicke assembly of the Church, for the exercise of Gods worship.

And that doth comprehend both the meditation of Gods word, and solemne prayers: and also the administration of the Sacramentes, and the exercise of the workes of mercie.

The exercise of the workes of mercie hath three partes, both the giuing of almes, and also the visiting of those that neede comfort, and also the helping of those that neede our helpe.

The giuing of almes is to be done for the helping and releeuing of the poore, of the sicke, of the prisoners, of the captiues, of those that suffer burnings, or shipwracks, and others that neede.

The visiting of those that neede comfort, is that of the orphans & widowes, in their affliction. Iam. 1.27.

The helping of those that neede our helpe and aide, is that of the sicke, of those that are besiedged, of captiues, or those that are in other dangers of life. Matt. 12.

Hitherto concerning the sanctification of an holy day: now concerning a godly fast.

A godly fast, is the outward worship of God, when wee for a time refraine from all meat and drinke, the more feruently to exercise godlinesse.

The ends thereof are:
- 1 That our vnruly flesh may be (as it were) tamed with hunger. 1. Cor. 9.25.26.27.
- 2 That we might prepare our selues to conceiue and make prayers with the earnest affection of the heart. Luk. 2.37. Act. 13. and 14.23. 1. Cor. 7.5.

- 3 That we might wholely cast downe and humble our selues before God with true griefe of mind.
- 4 That euen by outward testimonies, wee might whet on both our selues and others to repentance. Ioel. 2.14.15. 1. Samu. 7.5.6.

A priuate fast, is that which any hath priuately set to himselfe, for priuate causes and necessities. 2. Sam. 3.35. & 12.16. Nehem. 1.4. Est. 14.2. Dan. 9.3.

A publike fast, is that which is generally appointed by the authoritie of the Elders and a godly Magistrate, as often as any occasion of times, and imminent calamitie due for our sinnes do so require. Iud. 20.26. Ioel. 2.12. Ion. 3.5.7. 1. Sam. 7.6. 2. Sam. 1.11.12. Est. 14.3. Act. 13.2.3. & 14.23.

So much concerning a fast: now concerning a vow.

A vow, is a solemne promise made to God, concerning some lawfull & holy thing, which is in our power, and acceptable to God, to be performed in respect of the thankfulnes that is due to him.

And it is eyther conditionall or absolute.

A conditionall vow, is a vow to which the condition of time, or place, or some other circumstance is adioyned, that so, that which is vowed may be performed or not performed, according to the respect of the condition.

An absolute vow, is that which is without all condition. Psal. 102.

And both these vowes are eyther temporary, or perpetuall.

A temporary vow, is that by which any bindeth himselfe to some thing, at the least for a certaine season.

A perpetuall vow, is that whereby any bindeth himselfe to some thing all his life long, as Psal. 102.

Hitherto concerning a rite common to the old and new Testament: now concerning that that is proper to either of them.

A rite proper to eyther of them, is either of the old or new Testament.

A rite proper to the old Testament, is either publike or priuate.

A publike rite was that which was done in the solemne assembly.

And it was either the Iewish sacrifice, or the obseruing of holy times.

The Iewish sacrifice was a rite instituted by God, that it might be a putting of them in mind of the benefites to be bestowed vpon them by the Messias.

And it was either expiatory, or of thanksgiuing.

An expiatory sacrifice was a type of the oblation that was to come, which was to be slaine for the sins of mankind. In Greeke it is called a cleansing: otherwise it is called a satisfaction for sinne.

And it was eyther propitiatory, or sacrifices of redemption.

A propitiatory sacrifice was that in which the whole oblation was burned, to pacifie & appease God: it is also called a whole burnt offering.

Sacrifices of redemption were such, as by which sinnes were redeemed.

And they were eyther a sacrifice for sinne, or a sacrifice for offence.

A sacrifice for sinne, was a sacrifice redeeming sins committed of error or ignorance.

A Sacrifice for an offence, was a sacrifice redeeming offences wantonly committed, or as we say, more sleight transgression.

Thankesgiuing offrings, were those which on the behalfe of thankes were offered to God for benefites bestowed. Gen. 8.20.

Thanks offrings were meat offrings, peace offrings, and the sacrifice of praise.

A meat offering, was a thankes offering, in which meat was offered.

The Priest did take part of these, the rest was burned with incense.

Peace offrings was a sacrifice, in which only the fat of the oblations was burned, and they did receiue the rest, whose oblations they were.

The sacrifice of prayse, was a sacrifice in which cattell were slaine, and drinke offrings were to be offered to celebrate and set out prayses due to the Lord.

Hitherto concerning-sacrifices: now concerning the obseruation of holy times.

Holy times in the old testament were either of some set dayes, or else of yeares.

1 Of some set dayes, which were either daily, in which a continuall sacrifice was offered: and a continual sacrifice, was a sacrifice which was offered to God daily, at Morning and Euening. Exod. 29.38.39.

2 Or, of euery seuenth day, in which the Sabaoth was obserued.

The Sabaoth was a holy day, which was celebrated on euery seuenth day. Exod. 20.8.

3 Or of Calends, in which the new Moones were celebrated.

A new Moone, was a holy day, which was religiously obserued the first day of eueuery moneth. Num. 28.11.

Hitherto concerning the holy times of a day: now concerning the holy times of a yeare.

The holy times of a year, are those wherein were celebrated either yearely solemnities, or those which returned after many yeares.

Yearly solemnities were those which came euery where.

And they were instituted either by God, or by the Iewes.

Those that were instituted by God, were either great or lesser.

Great, as the Passeouer, Pentecost, and the feast of the Tabernacles.

The Passeouer was a great holy day, which was celebrated the fourteenth day of the moneth Abib, for the continuall remembrāce of bringing the people of Israell out of Egypt. Exod. 12.1.

Pentecost was a great holy day, obserued in the fiftieth day after the holy dayes of the Passeouer, in which euery family did offer two loues of the first of the corne, for remembrance of the publishing of the Law. Exod. 23.16. Leuit. 23.15.

The feasts of Tabernacles were holy daies, which were celebrated the fifteenth day of the seauenth moneth, in remembraunce of preseruing of the people abiding in tentes whilst they were in the wildernesse, and to put them in mind of thanksgiuing for the promised land deliuered to them, and for the yearely gathering of their corne. Deut. 16.

The lesser solemnities were those, which were celebrated with lesse preparation.

And they were either the feast of trumpets or of expiation.

The feast of trumpets was celebrated in the first day of the seuenth moneth: of expiation in the tenth of the same moneth. Leuit. 23. ver. 24.27.

Hitherto haue the solemnities instituted by God himselfe bene handled.

The solemnities instituted by the Iewes, were either the feast of Lots, or of restauration or dedication of the Temple.

The feast of lots were set holy daies of the Iewes, and commanded and instituted by Queene Hester and Mordecay, & they were celebrated in the fourteenth & fifteenth daies of the moneth Adar, in remembrance of the most cruell counsell of Aman, for slaying the Iewes euery where, which was hindered euen by God himselfe. Est. 9.17.

The feasts of restauration, or dedication of the Temple, were set holy daies of the Iewes, instituted by Iudas Maccabaeus, & they were celebrated in the fift day of the ninth moneth in remembrance of the religion and the temple restored, which before was prophaned by the Gentiles. 1. Macch. 4.59.

Hitherto concerning the yearly solemnities.

The solemnities which returned after many yeares were two: either the sabbaoth of the land, or the yeare of Iubilie.

The sabbaoth of the land, was a solemnity comming euery seuenth yeare, in which they were to cease from tilling their fields & vineyards. Leuit. 25.

The yeare of Iubilie was a solemnity comming euery fiftieth yeare, in which all their possessions returned to their owne maisters, & the Hebrew seruants were set free. Leu. 25.

Hitherto concerning the publicke rites of the old Testament: now concerning the priuate.

A priuate rite was that, which euery one did priuately obserue.

And it consisted both in manifold purifications, and also in the obseruing of the differences of meats.

Hitherto we haue handled the rites proper to the old Testament: the rites proper to the new Testament remaine to be treated of.

A rite proper to the new Testament, is an obseruing of the holy daies of the new Testament.

A holy day of the new Testament, is either weekely or yearely.

Weekly is the Lords day.

The Lords day is the first day of the week, wherein Christians do make solemne meetings to exercise the publicke worship of God. Act. 20.7. 1. Cor. 16.2. Reuel. 1.10.

But the Lords day is celebrated in stead of the sabbaoth for 3. causes, 1. that it might continually call to remembrance the benefite of the Lords resurrection. 2. That the beleeuers might vnderstand, that they are freed from the yoke of the Law. 3. That it might be a difference betweene vs that are Christians, and the Iews, who as yet (but without cause) are addicted to the obseruation of the time.

The yearely holy day of the new Testament, is either the feast of Christ, or else of the comming of the holy Spirit.

The holy daie or feast of Christ, is that which Christians by the repeating and holy remembrāce of speciall benefits which Christ hath bestowed on the Church is celebrated and kept for the honor of our Sauiour Christ himselfe.

And it is either the holy day of Christ his birth, or of Christs circumcision, or of his passion, or of his resurrection, or of his ascension into heauen.

Hitherto concerning the holy dayes of Christ.

The holy day of the holy Spirit, is the holy day of Pentecost, or Whitsontide as wee call it, in which the memory of sending the holy Spirite is remembred and set before vs.

And thus farre concerning the worship of God: now concerning vertue.

Vertue is a serious purpose of the will to liue honestly, continually and constantly manifesting it selfe by outward ctaions. Or vertue is an enclining of the will to honest actions. Psal. 1.2. & 39.2.10. & 102.2.3. and so forward. &
119.2.5.8.16.30.35.40.44.47.57.59.60.69.70.77.93.106.111.112.115.117.121.128.141.143.153.157.166.167.168.173.174. Dan. 1.8. Prou. 16.1. Iob. 39.37.38. in which places the will or purpose of the will, is always distinguished from the actions themselues, proceeding from the purpose of the will. Tit. 3.8. 1. Thess. 4.12. Rom. 12.17.

For euen as true faith is not idle, but working and powerfull by loue: so true Vertue is not a bare affection of the minde, or a naked purpose of the will, but declareth it selfe by outward honest actions, and doth shine in them: from whence it is that all the praise of vertue doth consist in action.

Therefore Vertue is the worker of honest actions: and therefore also the honest actions, by a metonymie of the effect are euery where almost called Vertues.

To Vertue is opposed a counterfaite Vertue and vice: the former as disparat or disagreeing, the other as contrary.

A counterfaite Vertue, is a false or fained shew, a pretext or appearance of Vertue.

Vice is a purpose of the will to liue dishonestly.

Vertue is referred to our selues• or others.

When it is referred to vs our selues, it is either the desire of wisedome, or a zeale of goodnesse: & also fortitude, and temperance,

⟨4 pages missing⟩

Chastity is an abstaining from straggling lusts and al impurity and vncleannesse, whether it be in mariage or out of mariage.

To it is contrary, the counterfaiting of chastity and filthinesse of life.

Of filthines there are many kinds, as these, fornication, adultery, whoredome, incest, rapte, daintinesse, sodomitry, beastlinesse.

Fornication is cōmitting of filthines with a single person, that hath bene defiled, or with a harlot.

Adultery is filthines with a maried person.

Whordome is filthinesse with a virgin.

Incest is filthinesse with one of the bloud, or that is of kinne.

Rapte is filthinesse with a maid violently stolen, or taken out of her fathers house.

Daintinesse is filthinesse, when any is willingly polluted by himselfe.

Sodomitry is filthinesse of man with man, or of woman with woman.

Beastlines is the filthines of mā with a beast.

Shamefastnesse is an abstaining not onely from delights following lust, as vnchast and immodest embracings, kisses, songs, & conferences, or speeches, but also from thoughts, gestures, and signs of lust, as from immodest mouing of the eyes, &c.

To it is contrary, the counterfeiting of shamefastnes, & immodesty or shamelesnes.

Hitherto concerning continency: now concerning thriftinesse.

Thriftines is a moderating of costs and expenses, that so they may become onely honest and necessary.

To it is cōtrary nigardlines & prodigality.

Nigardlines, is to vse riches so sparingly, that neither due honour is giuen to that kinde of life wherein a man liueth, neither can he almost spare any thing out of his substance and riches, but trouble and hard labour.

Prodigality is a vice, whē any doth by litle & litle wast, & at the lēgth cōsume his riches, in vnnecessary & immoderat costs & expēses

Thus farre concerning Temperance: now concerning the care or desire of true glory.

The care of true glory, is a vertue through which we by honest meanes, that is to say, by true godlines and vertue, do endeuour to get our selues a good name among others. Gal. 6.4. The Grecians expresse it by one word, which signifieth an honest care of glory.

The hunting after vaine glory, whether it be by hypocrisie, or wickednesse, or vice, or sinne, doth differ from it. Mat. 6.2. Gal. 5, 26. & 6.3. & so doth the contempt of true glory, as that in the Epicures, who passe away their life as beasts, which nature hath made prone and obedient to the belly. And these mē are ashamed of a good name of godlines & vertue

Hitherto we haue spoken of vertue which is referred to our selues: now concerning vertue towards others.

Vertue towards others, is that which by outward actions doth spread it self abroad to the vse of others, or of our neighbor, as we say

Our neighbour is euery man, whether he be our friend or enemy, rich or poore· either domesticall or a stranger: and especially those which stand in need of our helpe. Lu. 10.36.37.

Vertue towards other, is either humanity, ciuility, & brideling of the inordinat motiōs of the mind: or else christian loue and iustice.

Humanity is a vertue, when any signifieth his good will towards men by gestures and conuenient words.

To it is contrary, lightnes & inhumanity.

Ciuility, is a moderating of outward manners & gestures, that so they may agree with nature. By an other name it is called a speciall comlinesse.

Ciuility pertaineth to Vertue towards other, for it cannot be exercised but amongst others.

To it is ioyned graciousnesse.

Graciousnesse is a vertue, when any doth so striue vnto the elegancy and nature of manners, and gentlenesse of speach, that he may be gracious to others thereby.

To ciuility is contrary toyishnesse and clownishnesse.

Ciuility standeth either in modesty and grauity, or else in elegancy of manners, and cleanlinesse of attire.

Modesty is that, by which we in the motion of the whole body, do shun those things which do not become vs.

To it is contrary impudency.

Grauity is that, by which any sheweth a comelinesse and a conuenient dignity in the course of his life.

And that is either in speech, apparell, or gesture.

Grauity in speech is either the right vse of the tong, or taciturnity & stilnesse of speech.

The right vse or moderating of the tong, is a grauity when we so vse the tong, as when neede is· we speake fitly and in place such things only as belong to the glory of God, & edification of our neighbour.

And it is either in serious, or merry spech.

Serious speech is when necessary thinges are spoken, and that so farre forth as pertaineth to the good of others.

Merry speech consisteth in pleasantnesse.

Pleasantnesse is a modest dexterity, or quickenesse in pleasant speeches, and comely iesting: the Greeks call it pleasant table talke.

Scurrility is diuerse from it: and lumpishnesse is contrary to it.

To the right vse of the tongue is contrary the abuse of the tongue, when any doth with his tongue speake peruerse things. Prou. 10.31. that is to say, when any abuseth his tong to execrations, cursings, blasphemies, or to lie, to spread abroad false opinions, to scurrility and filthy speeches; to slander, to seduce, to giue euill counsell, & so forth. To speake peruerse things, is to subuert the trueth, iustice, good maners, to deceiue, blaspheme, backbite.

Taciturnity or silence, is a grauity, when we cōceale things which might incur the reprehension of such as are able to iudge iustly.

And it is either honest or necessary.

Honest taciturnity is a silence, whē we abstain & hold our peace from speaking, thē especially, whē it doth not become vs to speak.

Necessary taciturnity is a silence, whereby without the hurt of our cōscience, we cōceale secrets, least they might be spred to hurt any.

Grauity in apparell or attire, is that by which we obserue in our apparell or clothing a conuenient adorning of nature.

To it is contrary, lightnesse in apparell.

Grauity of gesture is that, by which we do so gouern the outward gestures of the whole body & seuerall members therof, that it may appeare therby that the mind is well ordered. Gentlenes in speach is that, by which we shew our selues easie, affable, & tractable: otherwise it is called popularity, affability, facility, &c.

That in our meetings & conuersatiō, bringeth forth pleasantnes in our words & works.

To gentlenes in speech is contrary, ouermuch care to please others, and morosity or way wardnesse.

Elegancy of manners is that, by which we endeuour for excellent manners.

Excellent manners are those, which agree with the customs of the mē with whō we liue

Those customes are either of our own coūtrey, or of strāgers, in the vse whereof we must obserue a comlines, namely, that they be there vsed where they are of force. For they which bring strange customes into their own countrey with them, and by them set out themselues, they are worthily ridiculous, and indeede to be laughed at.

Cleanlines of attire, is that, when we carry our selues cleanly in attire and rayment.

Hitherto concerning ciuility: now concerning brideling the inordinat motions of the mind.

Brideling of the inordinat motions of the minde, is either of pride, or of anger, or of couetousnesse.

The brideling of pride consisteth in modesty, and submission, and also in docility.

Modesty is a brideling of pride, by which we iudge conueniently of our selues, and doe not despise others. Rom. 12.3.

To it is contrary, the couterfeiting of comelinesse and immodesty.

The counterfeiting of comlines, is a faining of modesty, whē any hunteth after the praise of modesty, with the deniall of those thinges which yet he in his mind doth either truely or falsely attribute to himselfe, and with the refusing of those things which he desireth, and doth priuily endeuour to obtaine.

Submission is a brideling of pride, by which we cary our selues inferior to others, who are adorned with more excellent gifts. Mat. 18.3.

To it is contrary arrogancy.

Docility, is a brideling of pride, by which we do so gouerne our mind, that we doe not through the admiratiō of our owne wisdome contemne the iudgements of other, but that we heare others quietly, and yeeld being conuicted with true arguments.

To it is cōtrary, stubburnnes in errors, & the abounding in a mans own opiniō, & rash presumption of knowledge, when any one doth thinke, that he knoweth that which he is yet ignorant of. It may also be called the opinion of knowledge.

Concerning which, there are many notable sentences, as, glory offereth violence to the trueth. And againe, glory is the hinderance of promotion. The rash presumption of knowing doth forestall the way of learning. For wil any man suffer himselfe to be taught, that thinketh himselfe to be learned? Many might come to the highest degree of learning, but that they do falsely perswade themselues, that they haue already attained to it.

So much concerning the brideling of pride: now concerning the brideling of anger.

The brideling of anger, is either a desire of cōcord & mildnes, or long sufferāce & quietnes.

The desire of concord is a brideling of anger, by which we endeuour as much as in vs lieth, to embrace & haue peace with all men. To the same vertue it belōgeth to turne away and remoue the causes & occasiōs of offences, discords and hatreds, amongst vs or others.

Also to part from a mans owne right.

Also to restore or set concord betweene those that are at variance. Matt. 18.15.

Also not to reuenge an iniury offered or done. Matth. 18.15.

To the desire of concord is contrary an vniust reioycing or troublesomnesse, giuing or taking occasions of troubles and contentions with others.

Mildnesse, is a bridling of anger, by which we deale gently, and without disordered affections with others.

To it is contrary cockering and wrath.

Long sufferance, is a bridling of anger, by which we bridle the preposterous desire of reuenge. And to this is contrary, slownes & desire of reuenge.

Quietnes, is a bridling of anger, by which we are made easie to pardon iniuries and mutuall offences. Matth. 18.21.

To it is contrary lightnesse and implacabilitie, or a mind that can not be pacified.

Hitherto concerning the brideling of anger: now concerning the brideling of the desire, or couetousnesse.

The bridling of the desire, or couetousnes, is either of riches or honour.

The brideling of the desire for riches, is called contentednesse.

Contentednesse, is that by which wee are contented with present good things, rightly gotten, so that also we quietly beare pouertie.

To it is opposed couetousnesse, a counterfeit contempt of riches, an accusing of fortune, and the loathing of our present estate, or things present.

The brideling of the desire of honours, is whē we are so content with our present state, that we do not affect honors that are not due to vs.

To it is contrary an inconsiderate & rash affecting of honours, of a kingdome, of lordship and principalitie, &c.

Hitherto concerning the brideling of the inordinate motions of the mind: now concerning Christian loue.

Christian loue, is a vertue by which we declare our loue towards other. Rom. 12.10.

And it standeth both in liberality and friendship: and also in a fellow-like feeling, and procuring of other mens good.

Liberality, is loue towards our neighbour, by which we study & indeuor to profit him. Or else, liberality, is that by which wee succour an other mans necessitie.

And it consisteth both in communicating eyther of counsels or riches, and also in performing of duties.

Liberality, which consisteth in cōmunicating of counsels, is when we do readily and willingly bestow our gifts and learning for other mens profite.

Liberality, which consisteth in cōmunicating of riches, is either almes, or boūtifulnes.

Almes is a liberality towards the needy, by which we through compassion ministring vnto them things necessary for their sustentation, do relieue their wants and lackes. Esa. 58.7.8.9.10. Psal. 41.2.

Bountifulnesse, is liberality in bestowing gifts or benefits.

And it is either meane or sumptuous.

A meane bountifulnesse, is that by which we bestowe some thing on one of poorer estate.

And that may be in euery one according to the measure of his substance.

A sumptuous bountifulnes, is called magnificence.

Magnificence, is the sumptuous bountifulnesse only of great men.

Diuerse from it is riotousnesse.

Magnificence is either publike or priuate.

Publike, when costs are bestowed on publike vses. And they againe are bestowed either on holy things, as are the gifts, or things bequeathed to maintaine the ministers of the Church, the poore and stipendarie Scholers, and so foorth: to vphold buildings, or restore them being decayed, for the erecting of Temples, Schooles, Colledges, Hospitals for strangers, &c.

Or else they are giuen for ciuill vses: or to preserue, increase, and adorne the common wealth: as the building of a Court, of storehouses, of armories, of market places, of mils, of wals, of fortresses, also gifts to nourish by yearely costs & expences, the poore, or souldiers, or others which profite the commonwealth.

Or for the honest recreating and refreshing of the people, as publicke banquets, such as Dauid made. 2. Sam. 6.19.

Such magnificence is commendable, if it be referred to the glory of God: otherwise it shall be a monstrous and execrable pride, as that of King Ahashuerosh. Est. 1.

Priuate magnificence, is that which is exercised priuately towards some persons.

So much concerning liberalitie in communicating of riches.

Liberalitie in performing of duties, may be called dutifulnesse.

Dutifulnesse, or a dutifull will, is that which doth shine in the giuing and performing of duties.

The kinds of dutifulnesse are gratification and hospitalitie.

Gratification, or desire to gratifie, is dutifulnesse, by which we helpe other that neede our labour, or desire our helpe, as when we do help any to obtaine health. Mar. 7.32. Mat. 9.2. or other necessary things whatsoeuer.

Hospitalitie, is dutifulnesse, by which we embrace with all duties of hospitalitie, pilgrims and strangers, and especially those that are banished for the profession of the truth.

Thus farre concerning liberalitie: now concerning friendship.

Friendship, is to performe that true kindnesse towards others, which we would haue them performe towards vs.
Friendship is either publicke or priuate.
Publicke friendship is peace.
Priuate friendship, is a mutuall and true kindnesse amongst good men, stirred vp by the mutuall knowledge of vertue, or by honest duties, performing all such duties as are honest and possible. And such was that betweene Ionathan and Dauid.
That is also called Christian brotherhood: to which pertaineth the vnitie of the spirite, or to thinke the same thing, to will and nill the same thing.
To this is contrary flattery, and hart burning or enimity.

Hitherto concerning friendship: now concerning a fellowlike feeling.

A fellowlike or mutuall feeling, is loue by which we are duly touched with the state of other men.
And it is both towardes the liuing and the dead.
A fellowlike feeling towards the liuing is two fold: pitifulnesse, or congratulation.
Pitifulnesse, is that by which we are moued to lament with others for their aduersitie or vnhappy estate, otherwise it is called compassion, as Luk. 19. Christ with weeping did pity the miserable destruction of the Iewes. So Paule sayeth, Weepe with those that weepe.
To this vertue also it belongeth to visite the fatherlesse children and widowes in their calamities, and to comfort them.
To it is opposed, a reioycing in euill, and want of feeling or affection.
Congratulation, is that by which we reioyce with others for their prosperity or felicitie: of which Paul sayth; Reioyce with them that reioyce.

Thus farre concerning a fellowlike feeling towards the liuing: now towards the dead.

A fellowlike feeling towardes the dead, is both mourning, and also a care to bury them. 1. Sam. 28.3.
Mourning, is that by which we bewayle the death of those, who in their life were deare to vs. 1. Thess. 4.13. Act. 8.2. 2. Sam. 3.31.32.33.

Care to bury them, is that by which wee honorably commit the dead to their buriall. 1. Thess. 4.14.

So much concerning a fellowlike feeling: now of the procuring of other mens good.

The procuring of other mens good, is loue towards our neighbour, by which as much as we are able we further and promote his good. Prou. 3.29. Phil. 2.4. Or else it is whē we helpe and increase his commodities and profits as much as we can.

And that doth respect both the good name of our neighbour, and also other commodity of this life. Exod. 23.1.

Hitherto concerning loue: now concerning iustice.

Iustice, is a vertue giuing to euery one that which by duty or desert, is his owne.

And it is either vniuersall or particular.

Vniuersall iustice, is that which we generally owe to all.

And it is exercised and occupied either in admonishing of others, or in prayers for thē.

Particular iustice, is that which we ought to performe to them to whom we are specially and peculiarly bound.

And that is either priuate or publike.

Priuate, which euery one ought to performe priuately.

And that either in his owne proper calling, or in fellowship with others.

In his owne proper calling it is both the lawfull obtayning of an office, and the care of that his owne office: and also diligence & fidelity or faithfulnesse therein.

The lawfull obtaining of an office, is when a man obtayneth some office by lawfull waies and meanes: he doth not buy it with money as the Popes buy the Popedome.

The care of his own office, is when any dealeth with the matters of his owne calling, and doth not thrust himselfe into an other mans vocation.

Diligence, is that by which we execute, as well as we can the labours of our office and duty. 2. Thess. 3.10. Rom. 12.11. Prou. 12.4.5.

Or els when we do our workes diligently and faithfully, that we may be the better able to helpe the neede of others also.

Fidelity, is that by which we in our office do sincerely performe that which we haue receiued or vndertaken to do.

Hitherto concerning priuate iustice in a mans owne vocation.

Iustice, which ought to be performed in fellowship, is eyther distributiue (as we cal it) or commutatiue and interchangeable, as we may say.

Distributiue iustice, is that by which we performe to euery one, things agreeable to the condition, state, and dignity of euery one. Rom. 13.7. Honor to whom honor, tribute to whom tribute. Rom. 12.10.

And that is either appertayning to house and family, or else it is politicall and ciuill.

Iustice appertayning to the house, is that which ought to be exercised and performed either in domesticall fellowship, or in the accomplishment of domesticall or household duties.

This standeth in the holinesse of wedlock, and right guiding of household affaires.

Wedlocke, is a lawfull ioyning together of one man and woman, for the bringing forth of issue.

The holinesse of wedlocke doth consist both in a lawfull betroathing of man and wife, and also in the duties of wedlocke or mariage.

Betrothing, is a firme & certaine promise of wedlock between two, before fit witnesses appointed thereto: by another name it is called sponsals or spousals.

Fit witnesses, are those who can testifie the things which are required in betrothings.

And those things are either consent of the parties themselues, or els that the persons be fit for betroathing.

Consent is both of the bridegrome and of the bride: & also of the parents, or those who are in steed of their parents, and supply their places.

The consent of the bridegrome and of the bride, must be expressed and plaine, because wedlockes are ioyned by mutuall consent.

Consent is made and giuen, either with condition, or without condition.

If the consent be made with condition, they are termed betrothings of the time to come, or deliuered in the future tense, as we say.

In which, if the condition made in the beginning of the contract was honest and pertaining to wedlock, & were not yet fulfilled, the contract is broken or become voide.

Such as are these conditions: to wit, if the parents shall gree: if a conuenient dowrie shall be giuen thereto.

But when there followeth companying, or lying together, they not expecting or waiting for the performing of the condition, that coniunction is iudged to be wedlock▪ because the persons agreeing together, haue departed from the condition.

But if the condition be strange, that is to say nothing at all pertaining to wedlock: or if it be filthy, or impossible, thē it is to be reiected by the iudge, as though it had not bin added: neither is the contract to be dissolued for it, although the cōdition be not fulfilled: as that so, craftie dealing & wantonnesse may be forbidden in deceiuing the poore & weake sex.

If the consent be made or giuen without condition, they are called betrothings, in the present time or tense, in which the wedlock by a verbe of the present tense, or simply, is promised, and there is euen then the true beginning of present wedlock.

Now both error and compulsion must be farre remooued from the consent of the bridegroome and bride.

Error is either of the person, or of the condition.

Errour of the person, is when there is deceit as in respect of the parties. As Leah was deliuered to Iacob for Rahel.

For this error of the person both the betrothings and wedlock may be dissolued or broken.

Therefore Iacob might haue refused or cast off Leah, but he vsed not the strictnesse of his right.

The error of the condition, is when one person knoweth not the state of another.

The error of condition is two fold, for either it pertaineth to the condition of houshold affaires, or respecteth the state of the chastitie of one of the persons.

The error of condition, pertaining to the state of houshould affaires, is, if a woman thinke the bridgroome to be riche, or noble, or to haue no children.

For such an error of condition, the betrothings or wedlocke, are not to be broken or dissolued, because such an error doth not at all pertaine to the essentiall things of wedlock.

The errour of condition, pertaining to the state of the chastitie of one of the persons, is, if any being ignorant, doth marrie her that is deflowred, or with child by another.

In such an error the iudgement of Moses is one, and the iudgement of the common law is an other.

The iudgement of Moses is put downe, Deut. 22. chap. which commandeth her to be stoned with stones that was defiled by another, which afterward (as though she had bin a virgin) was married to another, if she were accused, & the man asked a diuorcement.

The proceeding of the common law, is two fold: one before their lying together, another after their lying together.

Before the lying together be committed, this proceeding is to be kept.

First reconciliation betweene them is to be assayed, that he who of error married her that was defiled by another, may keepe her, especially if she be modest, & will afterward liue chastly. And this course also wold be obserued, because oftentimes great calamities follow diuorcemēts, of which both the iudge and the actor, must haue speciall regard.

But if the reconciliation doth not proceed, the diuorcement must be made.

For it is better to follow the example of Moses law, then other reasons. For although the iudiciall lawes of Moses doe not pertaine to our states and places, yet we see in them what God alloweth. Furthermore the example of Moses law doth more strengthen the consciences, then other argumēts: because by the testimony of Gods lawe, the Iudges are sure that they doe not contrary to the will of God.

But after the lying together, it is to be determined, that ye bridegrome or husband may retaine her, which before was defiled by himselfe or some other, whether hee married her wittingly or ignorantly.

And that is established euen in our newe constitutions and orders, for three speciall causes.

The first, that their lightnes might not be strengthened who willingly vpon euery and any pretext do forsake their wiues, by what meanes soeuer their mind be altered.

The second is, least through suspicions or some small offences, the innocent parties should come into danger.

The third is this, that secret faults may not be layd open, which is more honest and profitable to be couered: according to the saying, Loue couereth all faults.

And thus we haue spoken concerning error, which ought to be farre from the consent of the bridegrome and the bride: now concerning compulsion.

Compulsion also ought to be far remoued, for there is no consent or wedlocke, when the person is by force compelled to promise wedlocke, and in this behalfe or respect many hurtfull errors and offences fall out.

The consent of the bridegrome & bride hath bin handled: now concerning the consent of others that haue interest and right therein.

The consent of others that haue right therin, is either of parents, or of those who are in steede of parents.

The consent of parents is of necessity required: and the betrothings are to be judged voyde, if the parents gaine-say the same before the commixtion, copulatiō, or lying together: because the authority of parents is not to be violated or broken.

But it doth belong to the office of the Iudge to consider, when the parents haue a probable cause of gaine saying, and when there is no probable cause.

But after the copulation or lying together the wedlocke cannot be cut off or broken by the authority of the parents: because the question is not now of the wedlocke to come: and there should iniury be offered to the woman forsaken or cast off.

The consent of those that are in steede of parents, as for example, of tutors, is not required of necessity, but for honesty sake only.

So much concerning the consent which is required to wedlocke: now followeth what persons be fitte.

That the persons may be fit there are required two things: first, that they be fitte both in regad of age and also of gifts, necessary for house keeping or gouernment. 1. Cor. 7.36.40. Prou. 31.10.11.

A full age is required, as which cannot only giue consent to the match, but is also fit for gouerning of houshold affaires and matters.

Therefore, the betrothing of men-chidren vnder fourteene yeares old, and wenches vnder twelue, yea though it be made by parents or tutors, is not the beginning of true wedlocke, & it may be dissolued when afterwards the will of the young folkes doth not like, or commeth not thereto. Neither is that party which is vnwilling to be compelled, which hath not boūd him or her self afterward whē their age was fit for wedlocke, & they might be able by their own iudgement to determine the matter.

The second thing is, that they may be ioyned together, hauing either power to bring forth issue, or by the law of nature.

By reason of hauing power to bring forth issue, such may be ioyned together as are not vnmeet for the cōpanying of wedlock: namely those that are not gelded men, or in whom nature is not hurt, by bewitching or poisning.

Gelded men are those, who are altogether vnfit for accompanying of wedlock, whether they be such by nature, or whether they be made vnfit by art, as being gelded.

Such persons are not to be ioyned in wedlock, therefore also the mariages being celebrated, when after the space of three yeares, the coldnesse of a gelded man is tried, or in three whole yeare, the healing of the nature being maimed, is attēpted in vain, the Iudge may pronounce that those persons are free. Neither yet then is diuorcemēt made because it was not wedlock: and to the person which hath the sound force of nature there may be granted another lawfull copulation, and the same more fruitfull.

<u>So much concerning those vvho may be ioyned together, as hauing power to bring foorth issue.</u>

By the law of nature, they which are not of kindred in the flesh, may contract matrimonie, Leuit. 8.5. and so forward.

For these are alwaies forbidden to be ioyned together, vnlesse when they are compelled by meere necessitie, to wit, when there want persons which are not of kindred in the flesh, as in the first and second beginning of people, the former vnder Adam after creatiō, the other vnder Noah after the floud.

Kinsfolks in the flesh, are those who touch vs in the flesh. Leuit. 18.6. & 25.49.

Propinquitie or aliance therefore is touching in flesh, or neerenesse in bloud.

Kinsfolkes in the flesh, are those who are neare vnto vs, either by nature or by mariage: from whence there is a double aliance in the flesh that is either by nature, or by mariage.

Kinsfolks by nature, are kinsfolkes of either of our parents, father or mother. Leuit. 18 12. or else kinsfolkes by nature, are those who descend and come of the same stock.

Wherevpon also they are called cousins in bloud, because they are ioined more neare vnto vn by the society of bloud, and of nature.

Aliance by nature therefore, or consanguinity and cousinage by bloud, is the kindred of persons, which because they do arise of one stock, they are ioined nearer vnto vs by the societie of bloud and nature.

A stock is a person from which others are deriued.

And alyes by nature or bloud, are discerned by line and degree.

The line, is a discent of alyes by nature deriued from one stock.

And that is either right or collaterall.

The right line, is either of kinsfolks ascending or descending.

Kinsfolks ascending, are first the father and mother: secondly, the fathers father, and mothers father: thirdly the great grandfather, and great grandmother: fourthly the great grandfathers father, and great grandmothers mother: and all other auncestours besides.

Kinsfolkes descending, are first the sonne and the daughter: secondly the nephew and the neece: thirdly the nephewes sonne, and the neeces daughter: fourthly, a sonne in the fourth degree, a daughter in the fourth degree: fiftly a son in the fift degree, a daughter in the fift degree: & what other childrē souer.

A collaterall or crosse line is two fold: equall or vnequall.

Equall, is that by which alies by nature do equally differ from the common stock.

Vnequall, is that by which alies by nature vnequally differ from the common stock.

Alies by nature, in an vnequall line, are either superiours or inferiours. And both either from the fathers stock, or from the mothers.

Superiours, are first the vncle and the aunt by the fathers side, the vncle and the aunt by the mothers side: secondly, the great vncle & great aunt by the fathers side, the great vncle, and great aunt by the mothers side: thirdly, my fathers vncle and aunt, my mothers vncle and aunt: fourthly, my fathers great vncle and great aunt, my mothers great vncle and great aunt.

Inferiours, are the sonnes of those referred to the superiours.

So much concerning the line: now concerning the degree.

A degree is a differēce or distance of persons from the stock, or of one person frō another.

And that either from the stocke or among themselues vnder the stock.

But in euery person we must number frō the stock.

Which numbring is called a genealogie. For a genealogie is a discent of the generation, counted in order: and the same is so numbred, that so the stock being set downe, from which the accounting of the degrees is to be begun, aboue that stock his auncestors must be placed, and beneath the same the sonnes & nephewes are set, and on the sides are added, the brothers and sisters. For example.

- Aram.
- Thare.
    - Abraham.
        - Isaac.
            - Iacob.
                - Ioseph.
- Nachor.

The knowledge of a genealogie, is necessarie for the vnderstanding first of the account of degrees, and secondly the forbidding of wedlock.

The reckoning of degrees is required, that we may know by how many degrees persons differ, concerning whose consanguinitie there is question made.

And seeing the line is two folde, right or collaterall, therefore the account of degrees, according to the difference of the lines is two folde also, the one in the right line, the other in the collaterall line.

In the right line, looke how many persons there are, so many degrees there are, excepting the stock from whēce the account must be begun: as Ioseph doth differ in the third degree from Abraham, Iacob in the second, Isaac in the first.

Therefore the sonne maketh the first degree, the nephew the second, the nephews son the third, the nephewes sons sonne the fourth, and so forth.

In the collaterall line, seeing it is two folde, that is, equall or vnequall, the maner of the reckoning is two folde also: the one in the equall line, the other in the vnequall.

In the equall line, by how many degrees the one person differeth from the common stock, by so many degrees the persons themselues differ one from another.

Therefore two bretheren, or a brother and a sister, are by consanguinitie ioined to themselues, in the first degree, as Iacob is ioined to Esau in the first degree. So the same man is ioined in the second degree to Rahel & Leah.

BATHVEL.
- Rebecca
- Iacob.
- Laban
- Rahel & Leah.

IEPPHNNE.
- Caleb.
- Axa.
- Cenas.
- Othniell.

Othniel therefore is ioined in the second degree to Axa.

In the vnequall line looke by how many degrees he that is remoued differeth from the stocke, by so many degrees they differ one from another.

THARE.
- Abraham
- Aram
- Sarah.

Sarah differeth two degrees from the stock: therefore she differeth so many degrees from Abraham, and is ioined to him in the second degree.

THARE.

- Abraham
- Isaac
- Nachor
- Bathuel
- Rebecca.

Rebecca differeth in the third degree from the stock: therefore also she differeth frō Isaac in the third degree, in which she was also ioyned to him.

<u>The account of the degrees hath beene handled, now followeth the forbidding of wedlock in respect of the degrees.</u>

The forbidding of wedlock according to the double difference of the line, is also two folde: one in the right line, the other in the collaterall.

In the right line all kinsfolkes, both ascending and descending are forbidden from mutuall mariages, and that as for the order of nature, so for the reuerence of bloud. Leuit. 18.7.

Wherefore if Adam were at this day aliue, he could not mary a wife.

In the collaterall line, forbidding also is two fold▪ the one in the equall line, the other in the vnequall line.

In the equall line, although by Gods law wedlocke was graunted in the second degree: and therefore it was lawfull for the sonnes or daughters of brethren to contract matrimony betweene themselues: yet now by mans law they are forbidden within the fourth degree: that so Gods forbidding might be obserued with greater reuerence.

Iacob married Rachell his cosin germane by the mothers side, to whom he was ioyned in the second degree.

Othmell married Axa, to whom he was also ioyned in the second degree.

And the dispensations which do graunt a commixion in the degrees forbidden in the Text. Leuit. chap. 18. are not of force. For the lawes in Leuiticus, which forbid the commixion of certaine persons, are the lawes of nature and bind all nations. For God or incestuous lusts punished euen the Gentiles, who were without the pollicy & gouernmēt of Moses, and which also were before Moses. As the text in Leu expresly saith, that the Egyptians and Canaanites were punished for incestuous lusts: so Paul punished the Corinthian who had touched his stepmother, or had carnally knowen her.

In the vnequall line, wedlockes are forbidden by Gods law, in the second degree, because generally God would haue more reuerence to be giuen to the superior degree then to the equall▪ because these in the vnequall line occupy the place of parents, & children. 1. Tim. 5.4.

Therefore the brother ought not to marry his sister, nor the nephew his aunt by his fathers side, nor his aunt by his mothers side, neither the neece ought to marry her vncle by her fathers side, or her vncle by her mothers side.

<u>Hitherto we haue spoken of alies by nature or by bloud: now of allies by mariage.</u>

Alies by marriage, are kinsefolks, of one of the married parties, by reason of the mariage contracted betwixt him and the party neare to him in bloud. As Dauid is nothing a kinne vnto Ionathan, but because he maried the sister of Ionathan to wife, now he is become the kinsman of Ionathan.

Affinity therefore is a nearinesse of persons, which mariage maketh betweene one maried party, and those that are neare in bloud to the other party maried also.

By how many degrees is my kinsman by bloud, by so many degrees his wife is my kinswoman by mariage: as two brethren are ioyned in the first degree of consanguinity: therefore the wife of my brother is ioyned to me in the first degree of affinity.

The forbidding of wedlocke in the first degree of affinity belongeth to the law of nature. Therefore Herod when he maried Herodias his brother Philips wife, committed incest, because Herodias was ioyned to Herod in the first degree of affinity.

HEROD.
- Herod.
- Philip whose wife was Herodias.

So Ruben also sinned, because hee defiled the bed of his father Iacob.
Iacob.
Ruben. his stepmother Bala.

Therefore Ruben touched or knew his stepmother in the first degree of affinity.

Affininity is not extended very farre, for my kinsmen in bloud are not kinne to my wifes cousins in bloud. I ought to abstain frō my wifes kinsewoman by bloud, and my kinsefolkes by bloud ought to abstaine from my wife, but yet not from my wifes kinsefolkes by bloud. Wherefore two brethren may marrie with two sisters, for they are not hindered by affinitie. The father & the sonne may marrie the mother and the daughter.

<u>Thus farre concerning the betroathings which ought to goe before wedlocke: now concerning the duties of wedlocke or mariage.</u>

The duties of wedlocke consist in the iustice of mariage, and in the education of children.

The common bond of these duties is a naturall affection.

A naturall affection, is a naturall loue of the nearenesse of bloud.

Iustice of mariage, is either cōmon to both the maried parties, or proper to the one.

The common iustice of both the maried parties is, 1. that both keepe their mariage loue perfect and vndefiled.

2 That they may dwell together with familiar felowship, and louingly liue together, that their life bee not passed away with sadnesse, or they be compelled to seeke comfort abrode, whereupon they may easily incurre infamie or slander.

3 That they mutually loue one another without iealosie, least otherwise they get thēselues continual anguish of heart and do mutually giue prouocation and allurement to breake their faith.

Iealousie, is the suspecting of adulterie in the parties that are maried.

If it fall out otherwise, the maried parties learne and feele by experience many discommodities: so that it is either a troublesome or sorowfull matrimonie, or diuorcement followeth.

Diuorcement is a lawfull breaking off of wedlocke.

The causes of diuorcement are onely two: one adulterie. Mat. 5.32 & 19.3.

The other is a forsaking, that is to say, a malicious departing of one of the maried parties, & that without anie iust causes, but either of lightnesse, or vniust impatience, & suffering of the bridle of mariage, or for some other vnnecessary causes. 1. Cor. 7.15.

But in diuorcement there ought to be obserued both the maner of proceeding, & also the time after which a second wedlocke or mariage may be granted to the innocent person.

The maner of proceeding comprehendeth both the lawfull knowledge that the Iudges haue, and also the trying of reconciliation, or the pronouncing of the sentence

The maner therefore of proceeding in the case of adulterie, ought so to be framed, that the parties being heard, the accusation may sufficiently be confirmed and proued, so that the guiltie person may be conuicted.

If the person which hath offended be foūd guiltie, and the innocent person doth require that a diuorcemēt be made, the Iudge ought first to trie them both, and to exhort them, that they would returne into sauour & loue one of them with another.

If the reconciliation doth not proceed, the innocent person may not be compelled to receiue the guiltie.

But if the person accusing, hath liued honestly, and doth require the sentence to be pronounced, it ought to be pronounced thus: Sith the person which hath offended, hath by his wickednesse dissolued wedlock, the iudge by the authoritie of the Gospell doth pronounce the innocent person to be free, and doth expressie graunt him, that according to his conscience he may safely and godlily marie another.

But the condemned person ought to be punished by the ciuill magistrate, to whome it belongeth to punish adulterie, either by exile that the guiltie person might be driuen out of those places, where the innocent person liueth, to whom the other, to wit, the condemned persō, is to be esteemed as dead: or else by some other punishment, which the magistrat shall iudge conuenient.

<u>And thus the maner of proceeding in the case of adultery ought to be framed and ordered: the maner of proceeding in the case of forsaking, now followeth to be handled.</u>

The proceeding in the case of forsaking, ought so to be framed and ordered, that the petition of the accuser being heard first, there should be lawfull triall made. That triall or knowledge consisteth in this, that it may be tried, whether the person be rightly forsaken or no: whether the coulour of forsaking be not vsed to couer lightnesse or vnfaithfulnes.

For he is not a forsaker, who is absent either because of some duty, as an ambassador, or souldier, chosen by lawfull authoritie to go a warfaring: or else by the will of his wife, as if he be absent some where for marchandise, or about some other honest businesse: or be held in captiuitie: or be caried away, if namely the case into which the husband falleth be such, as it doth not change the affection of the wife, that is to say, if there be no such wickednesse committed, wherby otherwise wedlock may be dissolued. Furthermore after it is knowne that the person is indeed forsaken, the person forsaking is to be called into iudgement by lawfull citing, done and affixed in the publike place, that so he may appeare within a certaine time, set and appointed therefore.

If the person forsaking doth not appeare within the set time, the testimonies cōcerning the integrity of the innocent person are to be heard, & that partie is to be pronounced free.

<u>Hitherto we haue spoken concerning the maner of proceeding in diuorcement: now we must speake of the time after which another wedlock may be graunted to the innocent person.</u>

There is a two folde consideration of the time, after which another wedlock is granted to the innocent person, one in the case of adulterie, another in the case of forsaking.

In the case of adultery the time is not prescribed to the innocent person, after the thing is once iudged.

In the case of forsaking, wedlock is to be graunted, if it do certainly appeare, that the persō forsaking either is dead, or hath in some place by committing adulterie, violated mariage, or would not appeare though he had knowledge of the scitation.

Otherwise the person forsaken ought to expect: for it falleth out that euen after nine yeares, the husband sometime returneth, especially if any be taken in warre in Turkey, or other where he beholden by the enimies in captiuitie.

Hitherto concerning common iustice of both the maried parties: now of that that is proper to one of them.

Iustice proper to one of the maried parties, doth peculiarlie appertaine either to the office and dutie of the husband or of the wife.

The office of the husband, is first to defend his wife, Col. 3.19.

2 Decently to vse his wife in ornaments & other necessaries. For she is not to be vsed or intreated as a handmaide or seruant, but as a fellow, because she was formed not out of the feet, but out of the side of man.

3 Gentlely, if need be to correct and admonish her, not angerly and sharply, least she be prouoked.

The dutie of the wife, is first to be subiect to her husband. Ephes. 5.22. Coloss. 3.18. 1. Pet. 3.1.

2 To be chaste and shamefast, modest and silent, godly and discreete.

3 To keepe her selfe at home, for the good gouernmēt of her family, not to stray abroad.

Hitherto concerning the iustice of mariage: now concerning the education of children.

The education or bringing vp of children, comprehendeth both the duties of parents and children.

The duty of parents, is first to sustaine their children with food and raiment. 1. Tim. 5.8.

2 To bring vp their children in learning, & discipline or instruction of the Lord. Eph. 6.4. Colos. 3.21.

3 Moderately to vse their fatherly power. that they do not grieue their children, & prouoke them to anger. Eph 6.4.

The dutie of children, is both to honour their parents. Eph. 6.1. Col. 3.20. and also to agree among themselues. Psal. 133.1. and mutually to loue and helpe one another.

Honour towards parents, comprehendeth reuerence, obedience, and beneficence or liberalitie towards their parents. Leuit. 19.3. Matth. 15.1.

Mar. 7.11.12. Christ sheweth out of the fifth commaundement, how children should do well to their parents.

Ioseph is a singular example of beneficence towards his parents and kinsfolkes, who brought into Egipt, and liberally nourished, not onely his father, but also his brethren (by whom he was sharply and vngently entreated and sold) and their whole family being vexed with very sore famine.

Hitherto concerning the holinesse of wedlock: now touching the disposing of houshold affaires or matters.

The disposing of houshold affaires, consisteth in the duty both of maisters, and also of seruants.

The dutie of maisters is, first, moderatelie to vse their authority ouer their seruāts Eph. 6.9

And that is done two wayes: first, if the maisters do not grieue their seruants with oouermuch labour, and do alwaies remember that they are not asses but men: secondly, if they do quietly gouerne them, and also quietly chide them, when they haue neglected their dutie, least they be prouoked with ouer hard words, and that they remember, that they also haue a Lord in heauen, with whom there is no respect of persons. Eph. 6.9.

2 Bountifully to reward the labour of their seruants, least being compelled by necessitie they should steale.

The duty of seruants is, first from their hearts to performe the labours that their maisters commaund them. Ephes. 6.5.6.

2 To be faithfull in things commited to them by their maisters, that so they may keepe their goods.

3 To obserue the vprightnesse of maners, that the wife, the sonnes and daughters, or other fellow seruants, be not corrupted by their bad counsels.

A iustice as pertaining to a houshold or familie hath bin thus set forth: ciuill iustice doth now follow.

A ciuill distributiue iustice, is that which ought to be performed in a politick societie.

And that is due either to euery one, or to some few.

To euery one is due, truth, sinceritie faithfulnesse, gentlenesse, and dutifulnesse.

Truth is that by which we do constantly loue & embrace true opinions, we speak true things, and both in our speach and gestures auoide deceitfull concealings and clokings of matters.

To it is contrary lying, and a deceitfull concealing of the truth.

Sinceritie, is when the tongue and gesture agree with the heart.

To it is contrary counterfeiting and faining.

Faithfulnesse, is that by which we keep our promises and couenants.

To it is contrarie deceipt, and breaking of faithfulnesse or fidelitie.

Gentlenesse, is that by which we iudging iustly of others, do attribute those due praises to them, which they deserue.

To the same vertue it belongeth to take all things in good part, not to backbite our neighbour, and not to giue eare to backbiters.

To gentlenesse is contrarie, quarelling, or backbiting, a foolish credulitie or beleefe, suspition and distrustfulnesse.

Quarelling, is a malitious taking of some thing in euill part.

Dutifulnesse, is that by which wee with outward due honour, embrace and reuerence those that are our superiours, by age, state or gifts. Rom. 12.

And that either in graunting to them the preheminence of speech, seate, and euerie action: or in gestures meete and fit according to the circumstances.

Hitherto concerning ciuill distributiue iustice, which ought to be exercised towards euery one: now followeth that which is to be exercised towards some fewe.

A ciuill distributiue iustice, which ought to be exercised toward some few is two fold: thankfulnesse and submission.

Thankfulnesse, is a vertue by which wee declare that we are thankfull towards our benefactors.

And that againe is either of the mind, or of the deed.

The thankfulnesse of the mind is that by which we thanke our benefactor for benefits bestowed on vs.

And that is declared both in giuing thāks for benefits receiued, we holding fast the memorie of them, & commending thē amongst others, and by godly wishes praying heartily for the good successe of those that deserue wel of vs: and also in bearing a verie readie mind to recompence the fauors receiued.

Thankefulnesse of the deed, is when we in deed, that is to say, in gifts and duties, requite the benefites that haue bene bestowed vpon vs.

To thankefulnesse is contrary vnthankfulnesse, and an vniust and vnlawful gratifying for benefits receiued.

Thus farre concerning thankefulnesse: now concerning submission.

Submission is a distributiue iustice, which is due to the politicke magistrate by the subiectes that are vnder him.

And that consisteth in obedience towards lawes and in the bearing of publike burdens. Rom. 13.1. Mat. 17.27. & 22.21. 1. Pet. 2.13.

To it is contrarie sedition, stubburnnesse, a faining of submission, & a wicked bondage, especially in idolatrous and vniust matters.

Hitherto concerning distributiue iustice: now concerning commutatiue iustice.

A commutatiue iustice, is that by which we according to our couenant, keep an equitie in our bargaines and contracts: or else, it is that by which we so deale with our neighbour in contractes, as we would desire to be dealt with our selues.

Hitherto concerning priuate iustice: now concerning publike iustice.

Publike iustice, is that which the publike Magistrate ought to exercise to preserue in safety the cōmon state of the subiects. 1. Ti. 2.2.

A Magistrate is a publike person, lawfully bearing rule ouer subiects. Rom. 13.1. Or he to whom it is granted to cōmand by authoritie.

Publike iustice is either in peace or warre.

Iustice in peace, is that by which the commodities of the subiectes are rightly ordered and gouerned in the time of peace.

And it is seene in the publishing and execution of lawes.

The publishing of lawes ought to respect the prosperitie & good estate of the subiects.

That prosperitie and good estate doth not onely consist in businesses pertaining to this life: but also or especially in this, that in the first place the true worship of God should be of force, from which alone all true felicitie doth proceed. Deut. 17.18. 2. Sam. 6.1. King. 2.27. & 11.11. Psal. 75.11.

The execution of lawes, is a bringing of thē to effect, for the preseruation of the publike discipline. Rom. 13.3.

And it is two fold: the defence of subiects, and brideling of euill men.

Of the defence of subiects there are two parts, the procuring and conseruation of the good estate of the subiects, and the aiding of them, who haue iust cause against the iniquitie of others.

The brideling of euil men, is another part of the execution of lawes, by which punishments are inflicted on the guiltie.

In the punishment is vsed either strictnesse or clemencie.

Strictnesse, is that by which according to the strict law, or rigorous seueritie of lawes, & that without mitigation, the punishment for the sinne pronounced after a lawfull maner, is inflicted on the sinfull offender. Psal. 102.1.5.8.

To strictneste is contrarie impunitie, and tyrannie or outragiousnesse, or crueltie and ouer much rigor.

Clemencie, is that by which for iust & sufficient causes, the punishment is remitted or mitigated to the guiltie. In Greeke it is called ετιεικεια, that is, equitie. Psal. 102.1.

To clemencie is contrarie tendernesse and softlinesse, which doth not only mitigate, but euen dissolue the bonds of lawes: & crueltie.

In the execution of lawes there must be no partialitie or respect of person, which is, an vncorrupt execution of lawes without accepting of persons. Psal. 82.1.2. Chro. 19. Deut. 1.16. & 16.18. Prou. 24.23.

To it is contrarie, the accepting or respect of persons, which is to attribute iust things to vniust men, or rewards to them that deserue not the same.

Thus farre concerning the iustice of the magistrate in peace: now concerning iustice in warre.

Iustice in warre, is the administring of war with equitie. Luc. 3.14.

Warre, is a necessarie defence against publike violence, or a iust punishment for haynous iniuries, which is vndertakē with force of armes by an ordinarie power. Iud. 8.19. & 20. throughout the whole chapter.

Of iustice in warre there are two parts: the vndertaking of warre only for a iust cause, & the preseruing of martiall discipline.

The end of the second booke of the Definitions and partitions of Diuinitie.

To God alone be glorie.

TO THE GENTLE reader health in Christ.

GEntle Reader, if anie thing in these definitiōs and partitions of diuinity do not satisfie thee, know thou, that I haue performed therin, as much as God of his grace hath giuen me at this time, & haue ministred vnto thee matter also that thou with me mightest thinke vpon and labour to find out. In the meane while vse these things as I do, to the sanctifying of Gods holy name. And so farewell.